Woodcarving
made easy

Woodcarving
made easy

Cynthia Rogers

GUILD OF MASTER CRAFTSMAN PUBLICATIONS

First published 2003 by
Guild of Master Craftsman Publications Ltd
Castle Place, 166 High Street,
Lewes, East Sussex BN7 1XU

Reprinted 2004

ISBN 1 86108 289 4

A catalogue record for this book is available from the British Library.

Publisher: Paul Richardson
Art Director: Ian Smith
Production Manager: Stuart Poole
Managing Editor: Gerrie Purcell
Commissioning Editor: April McCroskie
Editor: Stephen Haynes
Designer: Maggie Aldred
Photography: Anthony Bailey (cover and page 100), Cynthia Rogers (book)
Line drawings: John Yates

Set in Frutiger, Novarese and Lydian Cursive

Colour origination by P. T. Repro Warna (Indonesia)
Printed and bound by Kyodo Printing (Singapore)

Contents

Measurements

Although care has been taken to ensure that the metric measurements are true and accurate, they are only conversions from imperial; they have been rounded up or down to the nearest whole millimetre, or to the nearest convenient equivalent in cases where the imperial measurements themselves are only approximate.

When following the projects, use either the metric or the imperial measurements; do not mix units.

Photocopying

The designs in this book have been printed with generous margins so that readers may easily photocopy them to the required size for their own private use; but please note that all designs in this book are copyright and may not be reproduced for any other purpose without the permission of the designer and copyright owner.

Safety

Woodcarving should not be a dangerous activity, provided that sensible precautions are taken to avoid unnecessary risk.

• Always ensure that work is securely held in a suitable clamp or other device, and that the workplace lighting is adequate.

• Keep tools sharp; blunt tools are dangerous because they require more pressure and may behave unpredictably. Store them so that you, and others, cannot touch their cutting edges accidentally.

• Be particular about disposing of shavings, finishing materials, oily rags, etc., which may be a fire hazard.

• Do not work when your concentration is impaired by drugs, alcohol or fatigue.

• Do not remove safety guards from power tools; pay attention to electrical safety.

• The safety advice in this book is intended for your guidance, but cannot cover every eventuality: the safe use of hand and power tools is the responsibility of the user. If you are unhappy with a particular technique or procedure, do not use it – there is always another way.

ACKNOWLEDGEMENTS

This book would never have happened without the support and faith of three men.

Thanks to my father, William Rogers, who never lost faith in me.

Thanks to Ben Flack, master carver of Brisbane, Australia for infusing me with the carving bug.

Thanks to Tom Williams for being there.

Special mention to Hazel and Brian Orton for their help and advice with the photography. The mistakes are mine.

Introduction

The purpose of this book is to make carving easier and more appealing to the beginner or novice carver. To achieve this, all the projects are laid out in step-by-step detail, with special emphasis on perspective, which is the hardest lesson to learn.

At this stage it is not necessary to be able to draw, as the designs are supplied in the book. Later on, if the thought of laying out your own designs is worrying, there are ways to get around this.

By starting with a very simple project and moving forward from there, we can together build the confidence and experience to give you a good working knowledge of the craft.

This book contains simple instructions, beginning with what tools to use, how to hold them and where to start.

Don't forget that all life is a lesson, and that we all learn as we go along.

To begin with:
- *you don't need to be able to draw*
- *you don't need to be able to create your own designs*
- *you don't need any prior knowledge of timber*
- *you don't need to be a woodworker.*

All you need is the desire to try.

Many beginners are frightened by the thought of having to carve the background of a relief carving smooth and flat. They have seen the ugly digs or pick-outs that can result, and this deters them from trying. The method used in this book avoids this problem altogether. By using separate boards for the front and the back, all the drama is taken away, and the wood can be carved with easy access to all surfaces. The background will be free of marks, leaving you to concentrate on the actual carving.

The projects included are designed to build skills as they are completed; you will learn something extra with each step. There is no need to recess backgrounds until well down the woodcarving road. By this time, the confidence and the skill to handle it will be firmly in place.

The longest journey begins with the first step.

Getting started

1 Tools and equipment

If you are starting from scratch, you may want to begin with only a minimal amount of equipment. By starting with the minimum of chisels and buying them only as they are needed, you will always know exactly what each chisel will do. It is frustrating to have a handful of chisels that never get used. Only buy good-quality chisels: they will last a lifetime, and they will hold their edge and polish easily. Any of the major brands of carvers' chisels will stand you in good stead. Pfeil, Ashley Iles, Robert Sorby, Henry Taylor, Marples and Dastra are all well-known brands; if I have omitted a name it is by accident, not preference.

Though I myself have not had the opportunity to work with flexible-shank chisels, use them by all means if this is what you have and are comfortable with. The only tools that I would *not* recommend you use are improvised chisels made from cut-down rasps and files: they are very dangerous because they may break unexpectedly.

Because my own tools are by Pfeil, I have used their numbering system to identify the tools in this book. Recent Pfeil tools have two numbers printed on the handle, such as 3/5 or 5/3; the first number denotes the shape of the blade, while the second indicates the width in millimetres. Other makers produce a similar range of shapes but use slightly different numbering systems, so if you are using a different make you should refer to the diagrams beneath photo 1.1 (by courtesy of Craft Supplies Ltd) to see the shape I have in mind.

A suitable starter kit for tackling the projects in this book need include only a handful of specialist carving tools.

Photo 1.1 shows most of the chisels that are used throughout this book. From left to right they are:

- V-tool or parting tool: the one I use is medium-sized, with an angle of 60°. Pfeil call this size 12/8; other manufacturers may call it a 5/16in no. 39.

- 3/5 gouge: this has only a slight curve to the blade, and is valuable for getting into tight areas. Other makers may call it a 3/16in no. 4.
- 5/3 gouge (1/8in no. 5) (not in photo): this has a similar degree of curvature to the 3/5 but is smaller in width.
- 5F/14 fishtail: this has the same curvature as an ordinary no. 5 gouge, but with a splayed end. I find the fishtail the most versatile of all the tools and recommend its use. Different makers use different numberings for fishtail tools; 14mm is just over 1/2in.
- 8/7 gouge (1/4in no. 8); this is a very versatile gouge and can handle both small and large projects easily.
- 9/10 gouge (3/8in no. 9): definitely the best one to take any heavy grunt and get at all those dips and hollows.
- carving knife: any carving knife that has a straight blade will be fine here; we will not require the blade to be very flexible, so opt for safety.

A few auxiliary tools will also be needed:
- carving mallet
- 10in (255mm) bastard file
- leather strop for polishing chisels
- oilstone and honing oil
- slipstone.

A carver's mallet is round (both handle and head), so that no matter how you pick it up it will always be facing the right way to the chisel. My own personal mallet weighs 1lb 4oz (600g), but find one that you feel comfortable using; be aware that it is very tiring to use a heavy mallet over long periods. Never use a hammer to hit your chisels, as it will split and deform the handles in no time.

The sharpening equipment, and the method of using it, is discussed in the next chapter.

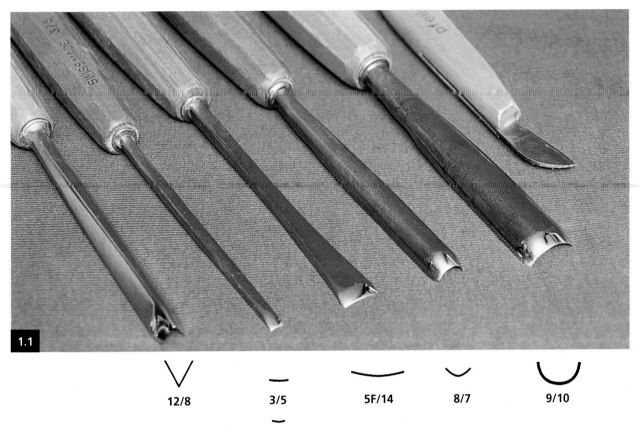

1.1

V
12/8

—
3/5

‿
5F/14

‿
8/7

U
9/10

—
5/3 (not shown)

1.2 Here you see some very common workshop and kitchen tools; from the left, they are:
• an old but clean paintbrush for dusting small fragments from your work
• a brass wire brush, which I use both to clean the file and to score fine hairs in animal carvings
• an ordinary teaspoon that gets used to gouge and shape the clay when making a preliminary model
• an old, blunt knife: vegetable knife, bread and butter knife or similar
• a stainless steel 6in (150mm) ruler for measuring the depth of the model
• pencil
• piece of chalk

1.2

- carpenter's square
- at rear, steel wool, grade 000 or 0000, for rubbing down the grain as you approach the finish
- at front, a 10in (255mm) bastard file.

There are other useful items which are not specific to carving, and you may already have some of them:
- sandpaper, cloth-backed, at least 180, 240, 320 and 400 grits
- two G-cramps (C-clamps), medium or large size
- dust mask
- wooden skewers, or thin kebab sticks
- non-skid mat or old towel, to stop tools rolling on the floor.

For drawing the design, and making a preliminary model of it, you will need the following. Most of these are familiar household articles which you probably already have:
- carbon paper, black (blue will leave dye on wood)
- modelling material such as Plasticine, or clay or modelling wax: about 3lb or 1.5kg. If using clay, then 325 (hand-building clay) is recommended
- ice-cream container plus spare lid, or a piece of non-porous board
- piece of chipboard (not MDF, which is denser and more likely to damage your cutting edges), large enough to go under the carving
- food wrap or plastic bag – a rubbish bag is best
- pencils, black and red
- chalk
- old vegetable-paring knife or similar.

The requirements for mixing and applying stains and finishes are simple:
- teaspoon
- three assorted soft-haired brushes for applying woodstain
- one medium-soft brush for applying oil
- old clean cloths for applying oil or rubbing stain
- variety of timber stains
- eyedropper
- Danish oil.

Finally, some basic tools are needed for initial preparation of the timber:
- ruler or tape measure
- carpenter's square, or plastic set square
- electric or hand drill and $1/32$, $1/8$ and $1/4$in (0.8, 3 and 6mm) drills
- bandsaw or handsaw for straight cuts
- scrollsaw, coping saw or fretsaw for curved cuts.

Choosing the timber

A list of timbers is given at the back of the book (page 144), but there are no fixed rules on what can be used. In the project chapters I describe the woods chosen for individual projects.

Work with decent wood; it will save a lot of frustration and disappointment, besides being easier to work with and saving you time and effort. Remember the old saying about not being able to make a silk purse out of a sow's ear.

Ask at a local club where you can find a merchant near you. They will be happy to help you and supply you with information on what timbers are suitable, depending on where you live and what is available. Alternatively, look in a woodcarving magazine for a club or merchant near you.

Lime, white beech, jelutong, basswood and camphor laurel are only a few of the well-liked carving timbers. All of these carve well, hold the detail, do not crumble easily, and are suitable for the novice or for the experienced carver. Do not buy wood just because it is cheap!

If you have done some carving and have a favourite wood, then use it by all means. Don't forget, even the plainest of wood can be improved by the use of stain.

Whatever timber you decide on, take care when laying out the project. Do not lay the design down just anywhere on the face of the wood. It is essential to consider the lie of the grain, and not just think of how much can be cut from your slab of wood; all will be lost if the grain runs at an angle across the design. The grain will show up even more clearly when the wood is oiled or polished. For my projects, the recommended grain direction is indicated on the working drawings.

Some things must be decided at the very start of each project, before any wood is cut. Put ideas down on paper and draw them up full scale; this is the time to make any necessary adjustments. Make a tracing of the design, either with tracing paper or waxed lunch wrap (greaseproof paper).

Decide whether the same timber is to be used for the backing board. If so, then the grain direction of the carving and the backing must either run parallel with each other or contrast. Be careful at this point: it will not look good when it's finished if the background grain is vertical and the carving in front is lying at an obtuse angle. The grain of the front carved piece should either be the same as the back or at right angles to it.

If both boards are to be matching, then care must be taken where the tracing is positioned. Decide where the outline of the backing will be, and take note of the grain. If it is to look like one piece when it is finished, you must position the tracing for the design so that the grain matches the backing. More timber may be used this way, but the results are well worth it.

Check for cracks or splits, and mark them with a contrasting-coloured pencil so they can be seen clearly. I would not be happy to find a split in the centre of the cut design – by marking the faults in this way, they can be seen through the tracing paper and avoided.

If you are cutting both front and back from the same board, make sure that you mark out where the backing is being cut from. This way the grain can be matched up more easily, especially when the design is on tracing paper so you can see through it.

Do not use a marker pen or highlighter to mark the timber, as many of the softer woods will absorb the dye and it will not come out.

Preparing the timber

Time spent in preparing the timber will save frustration, energy and headaches later.

The easiest way is to get the plank planed on a bench planer or put through a thicknesser. Local joineries will often do this (if a local club doesn't have the facilities), or there may be a business that allows you to hire the machinery by the hour and do it yourself on site, provided you are competent to use the equipment. Either way, the plank has to be dead flat. When you come to fit the back of the carved face to its backing board, there will be a problem if either one or both of these surfaces are not absolutely flat.

Regardless of whether the same or contrasting timbers are used, both boards will have to be planed first. Hand planers are available, but it can be hard to get a perfectly flat finish even using these. At least one surface of the carving timber will need to be put over the planer, while both faces of the backing board will need to be planed. By all means use a handplane if you have one.

Why plane only one face of the carving timber? Only the back face of the carved wood will touch the backing; the other face will be carved, and it only needs to be smooth enough to take a traced image. The backing, however, has to be planed both sides: one to match the back of the carving and one to leave a nice, smooth, clean surface on the back of the finished piece.

Run a straightedge over any timber to check that the faces are level, and always check at more than one place on the board – it may be flat one end and not the other, or may have a bow in it. Do not trust that the eye is good enough to pick out the differences. This must be done with every board.

Grain

Lie of the grain refers to the direction in which the grain runs.

Against the grain can be confusing, as at times it is hard to see the difference. Think of it as being like dog hair. **With** the grain, the hair lies flat and smooth; **against** the grain it stands up, and is spiky and hard to control.

Clean hands

It sounds ridiculous to say that clean hands are needed to be a woodcarver. However, hands have oils on them and timbers will show up these stains; they may defy removal, especially in pale timbers.

Blood is another thing that is hard to remove: if you get a scratch, then apply a dressing, or the stain may never come out of the wood.

Workshop safety

Let's start at the bottom and work up.

- Wear sensible shoes that cover the feet, not thongs or sandals. If a chisel were to be dropped, the blade could cut your foot badly.
- Make sure that any mats or duckboards are safe, with no turn-ups on the edges to trip over.
- Do not leave power leads in loose coils, or lying where they can be tripped over.
- Wear an apron to control loose clothing.
- If your hair is long, then confine it under a hat.
- Do not have electric leads lying on the bench top where it is possible to cut into them.
- Check the area again for safety.

The working area

1.3 Spread a non-slip mat or towel on the worktop to stop chisels from rolling onto the floor. This also stops them from striking the hard top of the workbench and dulling the blade. Spread the chisels in use on the towel, back from the edge of the bench and with the blades facing away from you. They will be easy to see and you will not stab yourself as you reach for them. Only the chisels in use should be on the worktop; the others are best in a rack of some kind.

Have good lighting above the work area: it's safer and makes it easier to work. Adjustable lamps are particularly helpful.

Make sure that the workbench is at a comfortable height for you. It should not be so high that you struggle to reach across it, or so low as to give you backache while you work. I find that just above waist height is pretty fair. The size of the bench depends on what you are likely to be carving, but it is better to have lots of room to work than to be cramped, not only for ease and access but safety also.

It goes without saying that a workbench needs to be strong and rigid, capable of having devices clamped to it and not liable to wobble while work is in progress.

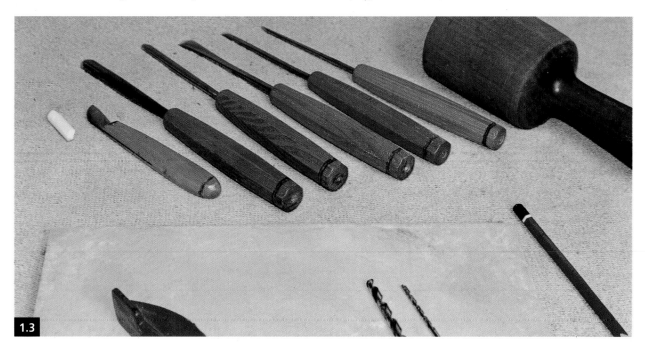

1.3

2 Sharpening

Blunt tools are not only harder to work with, but they will often tear the wood or not cut at all. It is in the best interests of the carver to keep chisels sharp and polished at all times – it's much easier to 'touch up' a blade from time to time than have to rehone it from scratch.

Pick up the gouges and look at the shape of each one. Because each has a different arc or curvature, each one must be held differently during sharpening for the whole cutting edge to be polished. When gouges are sharpened on a stone, the bevel of the blade must be allowed to complete a full sweep, or a flat spot will be left.

Honing oil (not ordinary lubricating oil) is used at all times on an oilstone; if using a diamond stone, then use water as lubricant. I personally use a hard Arkansas stone and honing oil, and find that it is easy to use and gives an excellent result.

Photo 2.1 The chisels have been pushed straight into a piece of jelutong to show their profiles; these are all the tools used in the projects in this book. The number of each chisel (in the system used by Pfeil of Switzerland) has been written alongside to make it easy to identify them.

Now consider the effects if a deep gouge like the 9/10 was put over the oilstone while being held in a position appropriate for the much shallower fishtail. The corners of the cutting edge would not be properly sharpened, while the centre could even be ground away. Think of a pendulum: if the swing of a pendulum was the same shape as the 9/10 gouge, it would travel a quite different path from that of the 5/14 fishtail.

The only part of the blade that will be sharpened is where it is in contact with the stone; this is why the angle is so important.

2.2 and 2.3 Take notice of the angle of the blade against the stone. The blade is being held with its bevel flat on the stone, and this is the angle at which the handle must be held for this blade to be sharpened. The bevel of the chisel is kept in this position by pushing down and forward with the left hand, while rolling the chisel with the other hand to conform to the contour.

2.4 A simple way to keep control of the arc is by moving the chisel in a figure-of-eight pattern over the oilstone (keeping the handle at the correct angle). In the photograph you can see clearly how the 9/10 has made a pattern in the oil as it is being rolled through the figure of eight; the angle of the sweep is also shown. By 'sweep' I am referring to the

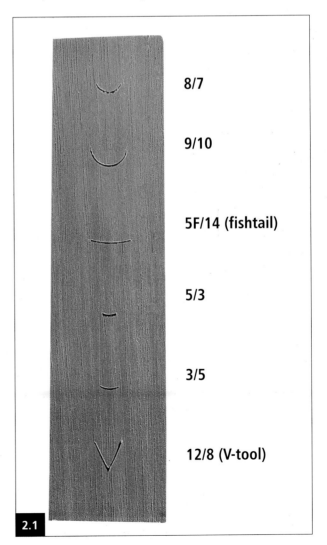

8/7

9/10

5F/14 (fishtail)

5/3

3/5

12/8 (V-tool)

2.1

9

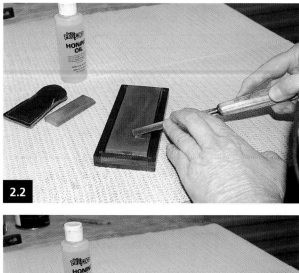

2.2

2.3

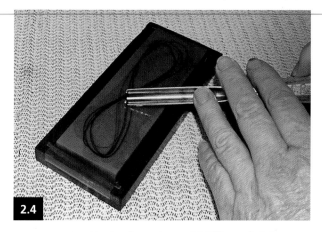

2.4

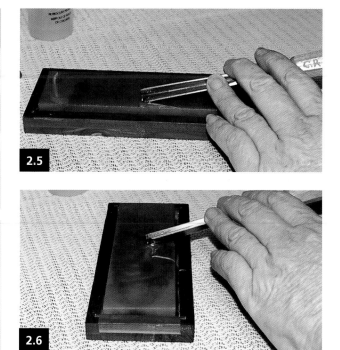

2.5

2.6

2.5 and 2.6 V-tools are sharpened in three sections. The flat faces are laid level on the stone and pushed with an even pressure back and forth, taking care not to roll them or turn them in any way. After both flat faces have been sharpened, the centre face (the tip of the V) is sharpened in the manner of a gouge, by rolling in short, tight figures of eight.

Over-honing the V results in the loss of the tip; not honing the tip of the V enough causes a parrot beak to form on the tip of the chisel. Both of these are the result of poor sharpening techniques.

2.7 The slipstone is used after honing to remove any slight burr that may be on the inside of the edge of the chisel. Dip the edge of the slipstone into clean

2.7

rotation of both of the hand and wrist, and of the chisel as it follows the contour of the figure of eight; this action should be fluid at all times.

The chisel is kept in contact with the stone throughout the sharpening process; do not lift it off the stone at any part of the sweep. Lifting would interrupt the even pressure that honing requires, and cause flat spots on the bevel.

Only flat chisels (as opposed to gouges) are kept flat to the oilstone, and not rotated.

honing oil and place it an inch (25mm) or so inside the chisel and back from the tip. Draw the stone along the channel of the chisel, out in a straight line past the tip.

Do not push the stone into the chisel (towards the handle), as this can cause chipping of the blade. Do not use a slipstone without oil.

A good-quality stone will keep the cutting edge on your chisels throughout their lifetime. After honing, buff them on leather to polish to a high sheen; oil or rouge is used on the leather for buffing.

Power sharpening

Electric wet-stone grinders do have a place in the workshop. Only use the stone wheel while it has water running over it, or the heat will ruin the temper of the chisel. Grinders are not recommended for the novice: more damage can be done in a few minutes with an electric grinder than in a year of bad hand-sharpening on an oilstone.

2.8 and 2.9 A buffing or polishing wheel made of leather is most useful, providing that the angle of the chisel is correct.

The machine is switched off for clarity in the photographs; note that when in motion, at all times the wheel must rotate *away from* the user. This way the chisels will not dig into the surface, but will be polished as the leather passes the face.

In these two photographs the flat on the side of the leather wheel is being used to polish the gouge to the correct contour. The tool still needs to be held at the correct angle. Use only that part of the buffing wheel whose shape matches the bevel of the particular chisel or gouge. The gouge will still require some rotation to work over its entire cutting edge.

2.10 and 2.11 Here the hollow or dip of the wheel is needed to get the right profile for the 9/10 and 8/7 gouges. The hand is turned to keep the chisel moving and keep the angle of the bevel correct.

Practice and patience are the keywords when it comes to sharpening chisels.

2.8

2.9

2.10

2.11

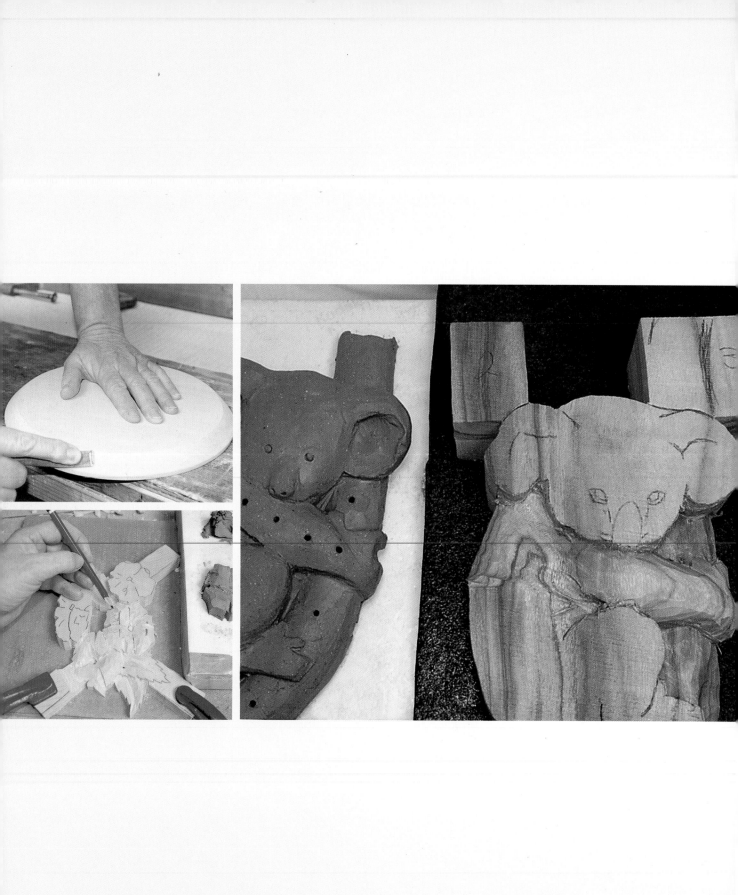

First projects

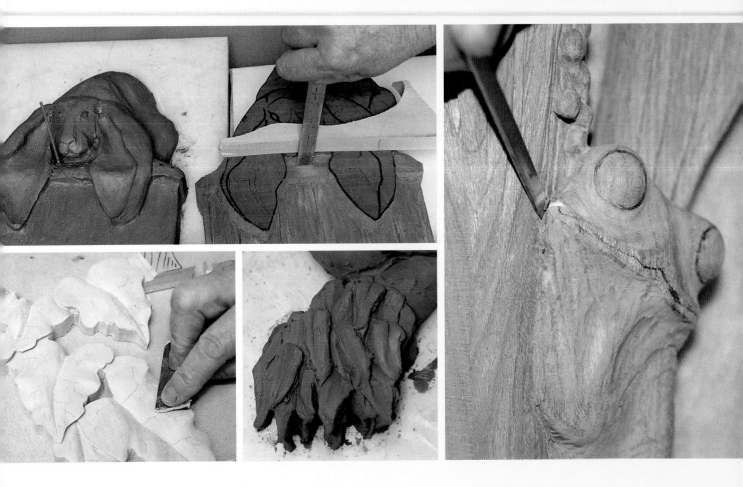

3 Foliage panel

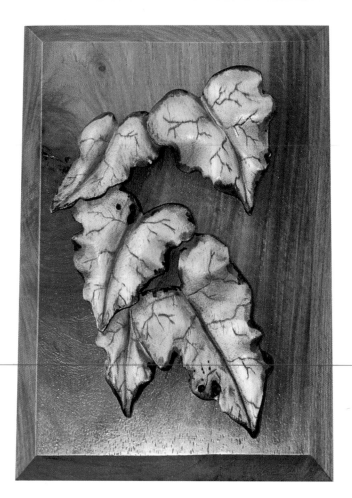

Preparation

There is no need to hurry; each person can set his or her own pace.

Photocopy the design to the size required; this is simply done at any newsagent's. Make two copies. If you choose to depart from the measurements given, be aware that very small designs are more difficult and fiddly, and the leaves are more likely to break.

For the carving I am going to use jelutong, which is ¹/₂in (12mm) thick, the board planed as discussed earlier (page 7). I find jelutong soft and easy to work, without being so brittle that it crumbles. It takes stain well, and it is not hard to obtain a good finish. For the backing some leftover rosewood is used, and this has also been planed. Any wood of your choosing will be suitable for the backing; be aware that rosewood is extremely hard, and may be expensive in your area.

Notice the 'tabs' drawn on the design. Be sure to include these when tracing and sawing, as the whole system depends on them. They are used to hold the timber while it is being carved, and they are not removed until the project is almost totally completed.

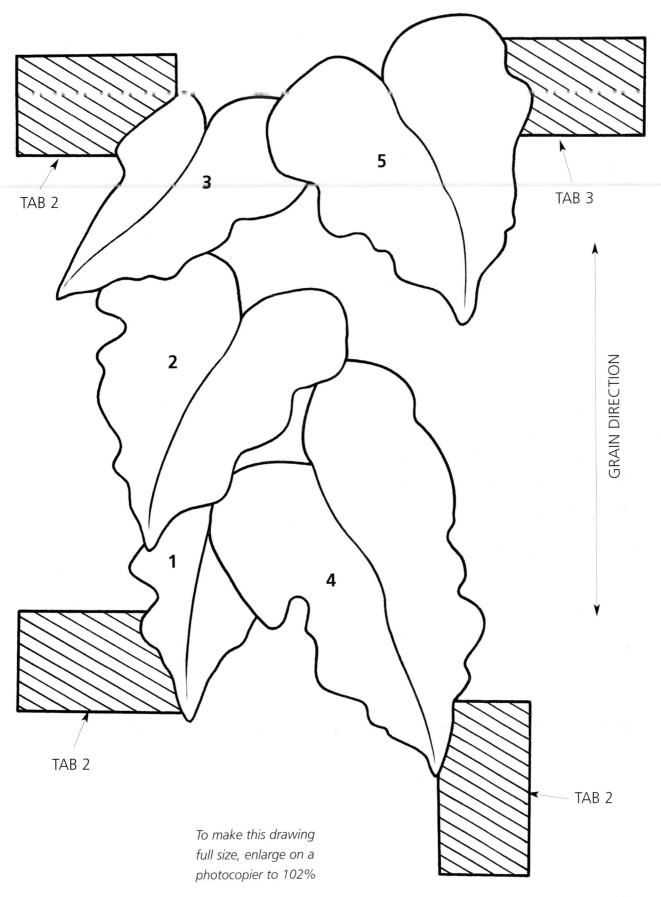

TAB 2

TAB 3

3

5

2

GRAIN DIRECTION

1

4

TAB 2

TAB 2

*To make this drawing
full size, enlarge on a
photocopier to 102%*

3.1

3.1 Decide whether contrasting boards are going to be used, or whether front and back are being cut from one board. Using a square, mark the board where the backing is to be cut, then carefully cut this on the outside of the marked lines.

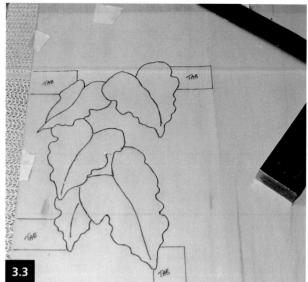

3.3

3.3 Trace the design and fix the tracing to the timber with masking tape. You can see through the tracing paper to align the pattern with the grain, or to avoid any faults in the wood.

Using black carbon paper, trace the design, including the tabs, onto the board. Remove the masking tape from one corner to check that no part of the design has been missed and that it has come through clearly. If necessary it can be gone over again with the pencil, but *not* a permanent marker!

3.2

3.2 If using a bench saw or a bandsaw, use a push-tool to keep your hands away from the blade – a spare piece of timber will do, and it will help keep the cut square.

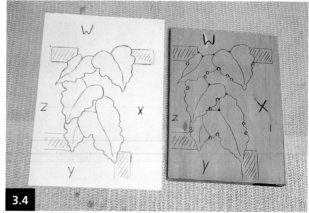

3.4

3.4 Before the design is cut out, mark the outer area of waste around it WXYZ, both on the wood and on the paper copy so it can be identified later. When you use the waste pieces later to test the grain direction, this will make it easy to find where they came from.

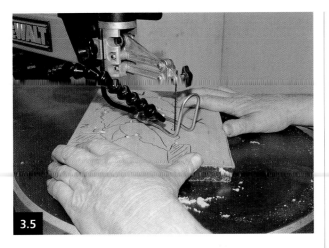

3.5

Cutting out the design

3.5 Now cut out the design, preferably on a bandsaw or scrollsaw. Don't forget to include the tabs, and make sure you keep your hands clear of the blade – even a scrollsaw needs care. Just go slowly, leave the tight corners at first, then go back a second time and do them later. If the tight cuts cause concern, then drill holes as explained below for the hand method.

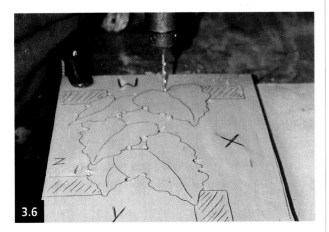

3.6

Hand method

3.6 If you cannot get your wood cut on a bandsaw or scrollsaw, then do it by hand. Using either a hand drill or an electric drill, with a 1/8in (3mm) bit, drill into the tight corners of the design where they have been marked in red in the photograph, clamping the board securely with a G-cramp.

Use the 1/4in (6mm) drill for the bigger spaces, until all the tight spots have been opened up. Do not worry if it looks untidy, as long as you stay outside the line of the drawing.

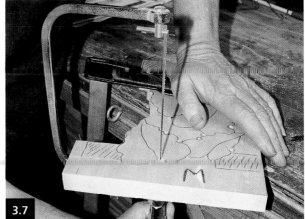

3.7

3.7 Now it is easy to cut away the larger part of the waste by hand with a fretsaw or coping saw, while holding it down with a G-cramp. It will not take very long doing it this way: jelutong is not hard and the design is not very big.

Preparing to carve

Stick a copy of the design to the wall or onto a piece of cardboard where it can seen, and for the moment put the saws and drills away. Put aside the cut-out design and put the backing away for working on later. Place a piece of chipboard or softboard on the bench and have a G-cramp handy. Before starting on the carving it pays to test the grain direction of the wood using the offcuts.

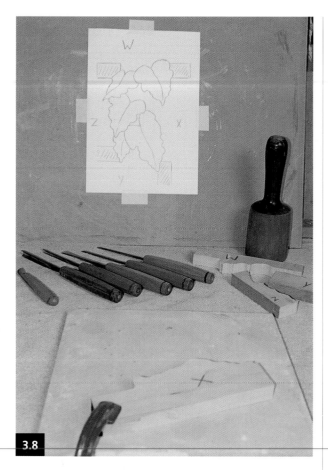

3.8

3.8 From the sections marked earlier with WXYZ, take section X and clamp it down securely with the G-cramp to the chipboard and the bench.

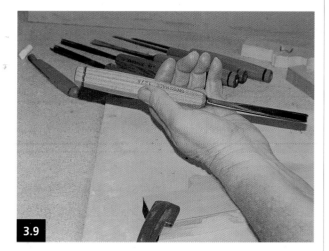

3.9

Holding the chisels

3.9 Take note of the way that the chisel is laid into the palm of the hand: to be ready to carve, all that is needed is for the hand to be closed.

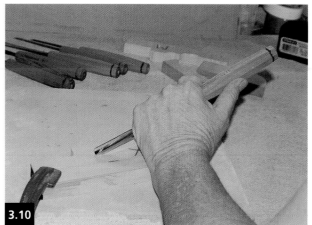

3.10

3.10 Total control is maintained at all times, no matter from which direction the cut is made; just turn the closed hand to right or left to alter the direction of the cut. The hand closed on the ferrule of the tool (the part where shaft and handle meet) acts as a stop, restricts unwanted movement of the chisel, and stops it from flying from the hand when it is tapped with the mallet.

By moving the wrist, the depth of cut as well as the angle can be altered; practise to get the feel of the chisel. Do not hold it in a death-grip – firmly enough not to drop it and loose enough not to tire too easily is just right.

Being round, a carver's mallet is always in the right position to use. It does not need to be very heavy. The timber we are carving is not like old tree stumps – all that is required is a nice sharp tap on the chisel handle. Do not use an ordinary hammer on the chisels: it will destroy the handles in no time.

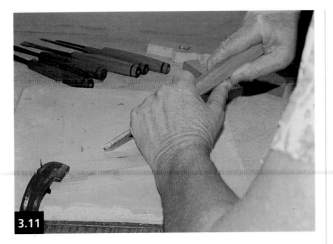

3.11

Carving the wood

3.11 Sometimes the chisel is pushed through the wood with one hand while guiding it with the other. Do not damage the palm of your hand by banging it on the chisel to drive it along; that is what you bought the mallet for.

3.12

3.12 The offcut that was clamped down earlier (piece X) was cut away from the right side of the design. Take the V-tool and, holding it firmly, push it through the wood in the direction of the grain. How did it cut? Try it a few times. Take care not to hit the G-cramp, or the end of the chisel will be damaged. Now try cutting across the grain at an angle and take notice of how it cuts. Turn the piece of wood around end for end and try cutting it from this angle. Which direction gives the cleanest and easiest cut?

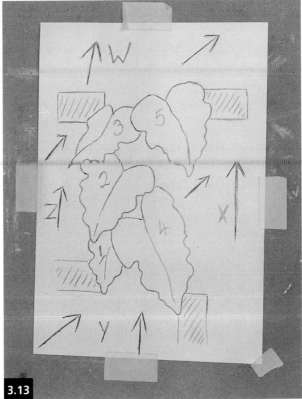

3.13

3.13 If unsure, repeat the whole test. When the decision has been made, draw an arrow in chalk pointing in the direction in which the wood cuts most cleanly and easily. Copy that direction onto the drawing. Try the other pieces, W, Y and Z, and mark their grain directions on the drawing. Practise with the chisels on the offcuts, get the feel of them in your hand and get a 'feel' for the timber.

Do *not* just copy the directions of the arrows in my photograph – there could be all sorts of differences between the timber shown here and what is available to you. Every piece of timber is different. It's possible also that we may be working from opposite ends of the plank.

Each time a project is started, it pays to make these test cuts so that you know *before* starting to carve which is the best (or worst) way to work. It saves many problems if you spend a little time getting the feel of the timber and the chisels first, using the offcuts as I have described.

Deciding where to start

The leaves have been numbered in the working drawing and in photo 3.13, and this is the sequence in which they will be carved. The reason is that it is easier to carve the leaves that have the lowest profile (the furthest from the surface) first. That way there is less risk of cutting the highest leaf right down low and then not having enough space or timber to set the lower ones beneath it.

Because it is hard to project or imagine a non-existent shape on a flat board, it is practical and easy to make a 'working model' of the project. The ice-cream container lid or the non-stick board (or plastic on board) and two offcuts from the design that was cut out is all that is required.

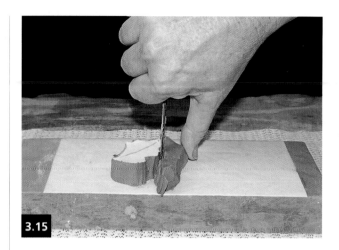

3.15 From the spare copy of the design (not the one with the arrows on it), use scissors to cut out the pattern of leaf no. 1. Lay it on top of the model, pressing it only firmly enough to make it stay in place. Carefully, using an old vegetable knife or similar, cut vertically around the paper pattern. If it squashes, just roll it up and start the whole thing again. This is now a life-size model of leaf no. 1. This leaf is the lowest of the group in regard to its thickness when it is carved, so it will be carved first.

Clamp the timber firmly to the waste board, making sure that it is positioned to allow access to cut in the direction of the red arrows. The design in the photo might be facing in a different direction from what you require – that's OK as long as you cut the way that the arrows point on *your* timber.

Place the model on the workbench where it can be seen clearly, but not close enough that it is liable to be leant on and squashed. The idea is that we work on it as we go along, to help establish the shape that is to be carved.

Cutting a trench alongside the design

The first task is to outline the design by cutting a groove along the surface of each of the tabs, just outside the final outline of the leaves. There are two ways to do this; I suggest you try both.

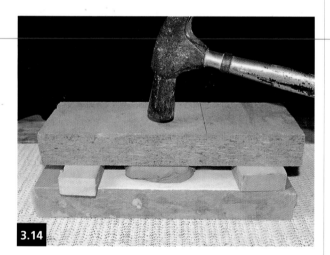

3.14 Take a small handful of clay or modelling material and place it between the offcuts on the board. Place another board on top and hit the top board with a hammer. Now the clay or modelling material is the same thickness as the carving timber; from here on it will be referred to as the 'model'.

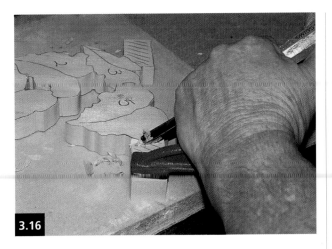

3.16

3.18

3.16 *Option 1* Take the V-tool and, cutting with the grain (check your arrows), cut a trench no wider than ¼in (6mm) along the outside of the leaf, following the contours without cutting into the design itself. Make this cut about ¼in (6mm) down into the wood, leaving a groove on the outside of the design. Do not cut the tab off!

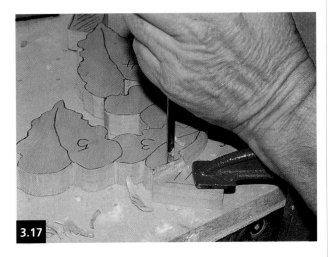

3.17

3.17 *Option 2* Using the smaller 8/7 gouge, cut a groove just outside of the pencil line of the design. Then take chisel size 3/5 and, holding it upright, push downwards (this is known as a **stab cut**) along the length of the design edge, turning the blade to follow the contours. If the wood is very soft, a gentle push is all that is needed; you should have the 'feel' of the timber from practising earlier.

3.18 Using the same 3/5 chisel at a lower angle, gently cut along the edge of the design to pare away the waste near the design edge. This will leave a definite edge to the design, but do not get upset if it is a bit ragged; it will be cleaned up later.

Modelling and carving leaf no. 1

A life-size model of the leaf about to be carved shows clearly how each action will affect the contour of the timber leaf. Making each cut on the model first makes it clear where the cuts are needed on the wood, and how deep to make them to get the effect required. It also helps to be able to see what each action will achieve before cutting into the wood; this allows you to proceed with confidence.

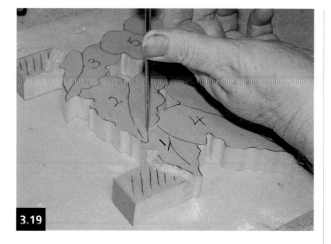

3.19

3.19 **Timber** Holding the 3/5 chisel upright and pushing downwards, make dividing cuts between leaves 1 and 2 and also between 1 and 4, turning the chisel to conform to the pattern shape.

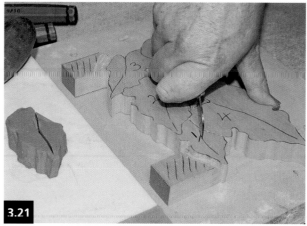

3.21

3.21 **Clay** Mark the centre vein with the knife. **Timber** Use the carving knife to cut the centre of the timber.

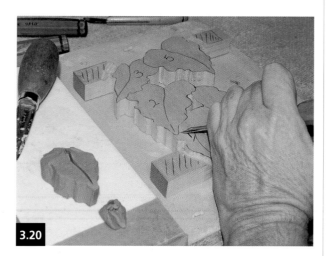

3.20

3.20 **Clay** Use the knife to lower the rear left of leaf 1, where it adjoins leaf 2.
Timber Using the fishtail, remove waste to match the clay by pushing towards the dividing cuts you have already made. Take care not to drive the chisel into leaf 2. Either push the chisel with your other hand or tap gently with the mallet.

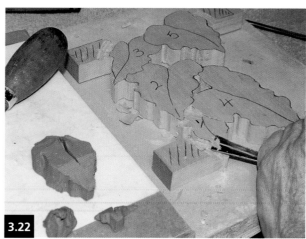

3.22

3.22 **Clay** Slope down the tip of the leaf, to about a quarter of its length.
Timber Use the fishtail to cut the same area on the timber. Keep your hand low and cut slightly across the grain so as not to induce splitting.

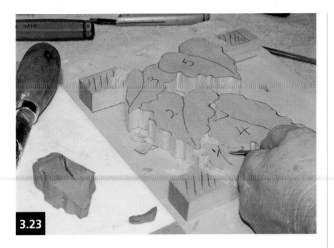

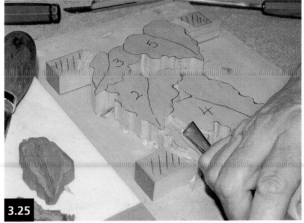

3.23 *Clay* Lower the right side, where leaves 1 and 4 touch.
Timber Using the fishtail tilted at an angle, cut away on the right to match the model.

3.25 *Clay* Cut down the right side of the centre line and remove material to leave a V-shaped valley.
Timber Turn the fishtail over to remove wood from right of centre, taking care not to cut into leaf no. 4.

Leaf no. 2

Go through the process of thicknessing the model material, cutting out leaf no. 2 and trimming the sides, as with the first model.

Holding the chisel as before, cut between the adjoining leaves where they touch, using downward stab-cuts.

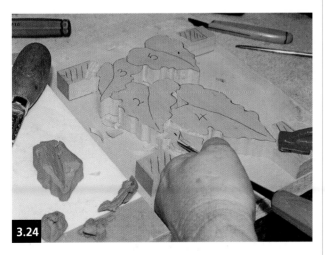

3.24 *Clay* Cut down the left side of the centre line and remove the clay from this section.
Timber Use the fishtail, tilted as shown, to remove the wood to the left of the centre line.

3.26 *Clay* Cut the centre line of leaf 2 – not very deeply at the tip.
Timber Use the carving knife to make the same cut on the timber. Hold the knife firmly to keep control.

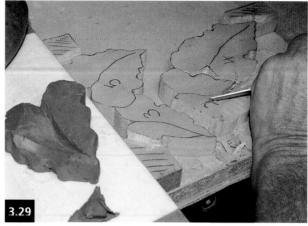

3.27

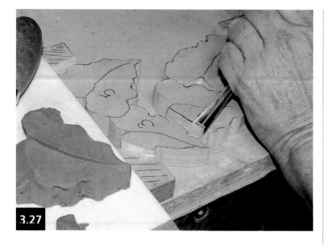

3.28

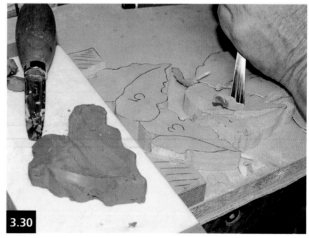

3.29

3.30

3.27 **Clay** Remove top left side of leaf 2, from the point corresponding to the pencil line on the wood in the photograph.
Timber Using the fishtail, cut towards leaf 3 from the pencil mark.

3.28 **Clay** Use a teaspoon to take a scoop out of the left side towards the outer edge.
Timber Using the 9/10 gouge, cut a groove in the timber to match the clay.

3.29 **Clay** Remove clay from left of centre, leaving the tip intact.
Timber Use the fishtail at an angle to cut to the left of the centre line as shown.

3.30 **Clay and timber** Cut to the right side of the centre line in the same way. On the timber, use the fishtail at a 45° angle.

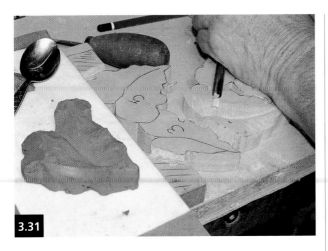

3.31

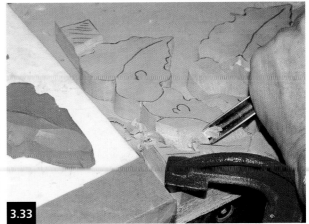

3.33

3.31 *Clay* Dig grooves with the teaspoon to make the right edge of the leaf wavy.
Timber Use the 9/10 gouge to create a wavy edge on the wood.
Finally, separate leaves 2 and 4 by cutting down along the pencil line.

Leaf no. 3

Stab-cut the line between leaves 3 and 5. Deepen the groove in the tab until it is half the thickness of the timber.
Clay Mark the centre line with the knife.
Timber Use the carving knife to cut the same area on the timber.

3.33 *Clay* Remove a large scoop from the left front edge as shown.
Timber Cutting from the centre line, use the 9/10 to make a similar scoop in the leaf.

3.32

3.34

3.32 *Clay* Bevel the outer left edge of the leaf.
Timber Use the fishtail to remove the same area of the timber, almost to the level of the tab groove.

3.34 *Clay* Cut away the clay to the left of the centre line.
Timber Use the fishtail upside down to remove wood from left of centre.

3.35

3.35 *Clay* Note in the photograph how the clay has been removed from the right of the centre line over the last three quarters of the leaf, but not the tip.
Timber Using the fishtail, remove timber from the corresponding area. The chisel is being used right side up this time.

3.37

Leaf no. 4

3.37 *Clay* Cut clay from the top edges of the leaf as shown by the pencil marks.
Timber Use the fishtail to lower both top edges of leaf 4 as marked in pencil.

3.36

3.36 *Clay* Lower the back edge of the leaf where it joins nos. 3 and 5, then use a spoon to cut a groove in the right side of the leaf, as shown by the pencil marks in the photograph.
Timber Use the fishtail to lower the back of the leaf where it touches leaf 5, then use the 9/10 to cut the groove that is marked behind the chisel in the photograph.

3.38

3.38 *Clay* Use the spoon to cut grooves in the clay to give the leaf a wavy appearance. The handle of the spoon can be used for the tighter grooves.
Timber Use the 8/7 for the smaller, tighter grooves, the 9/10 for the wider grooves.

3.39

3.39 **Clay** Cut the centre line with the knife and remove material to right of centre.
Timber Cut along the centre with the knife, then use the fishtail to remove material to right of centre.

3.41

3.41 **Clay** Rub over the surface with a spoon to soften the contours.
Timber To soften the look of the surface, use the fishtail to remove the hard, sharp edges. Work slowly and carefully, removing only very small amounts of timber where needed. This part takes time, but is worth the effort.

3.40

3.40 **Clay and timber** Remove waste from left of centre to form a V.

3.42

Leaf no. 5

3.42 **Clay** Cut the centre line and lower the tip of the leaf.
Timber Cut the centre line and use the fishtail to lower the tip.

3.43 **Clay** Remove waste from both left and right of the centre line.
Timber Use the fishtail to remove the waste.

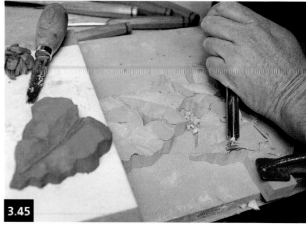

3.45 **Clay** Use the spoon to make large depressions on the outer right edge.
Timber Use the 9/10 gouge to create the same undulating appearance.

Sanding and undercutting

Many carvers do not sand their work at all; sometimes this is dictated by preference, sometimes by the timber. If the timber is very hard and close-grained, some carvers will leave a 'chisel' finish to their work. Because jelutong is very soft and somewhat 'hairy', in my opinion it requires sanding.
   Sand leaf no. 5 first.

3.44 **Clay** Gouge the centre left side of leaf using the spoon.
Timber Use the 9/10 gouge to lower the same area.

3.46 For safety, wear a dust mask while sanding. Work through the grades of sandpaper, starting with the coarsest and finishing with the finest. Roll the paper or double it as needed; this gives it sufficient strength and 'body' to enable pressure to be used, and saves wear and tear on the fingers. Wrapping the sandpaper around a lollipop stick or similar object allows more pressure to be applied without undue fatigue, but be careful that the stick does not protrude and damage the face of the leaf. Fold the paper to get into central areas and tight corners.

The minimum amount of sanding needed would be three grades of paper; some timbers require five to give the best finish. It helps to have a large, clean paintbrush handy to brush away debris so you can see more clearly.

3.48 Now lower the handle of the 3/5 chisel and cut forwards. This will sever the timber from the area beneath the overhang of the leaf. Carefully sand this undercut area with folded sandpaper as before.

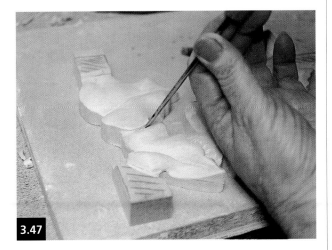

3.47 Now sand leaf no. 3. After sanding, take the 3/5 chisel and, holding it as shown, cut down at an angle under leaf 5. Take care not to lift the hand, as this will lever the timber, causing it to break – just push it forward and withdraw it smoothly.

3.49 Sand leaf no. 2 and, alternating with the 3/5 chisel as required, undercut leaf 3, again sanding the undercuts.

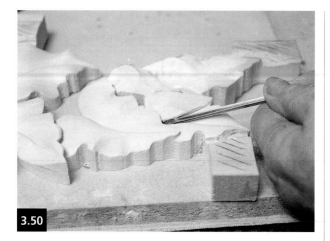

3.50

3.50 Sand leaf no. 1, working through the grades of paper again. When undercutting between leaves 1 and 2, take care not to lose the tip of leaf 2. The photograph shows how the angles of the undercuts all vary, depending on depth, shape or contour.

3.51

3.51 Take care when undercutting between leaves 4 and 2. Sand the undercuts as before. Notice that none of the tabs have been cut away yet, as we still need them.

3.52

Veining

3.52 The three leaves shown here are (from left to right) Kentucky climbing bean, acanthus and caladium. While these are not the only patterns of leaf veins, they show some of the variety that the garden offers. I suggest you pick or at least study different types of leaves before attempting to carve them in wood.

The different types of timber also present their own problems and require different approaches. It is relatively easy to cut fine lines with a chisel in hard woods that cut cleanly, whereas soft woods are inclined to tear. Practice is again important, especially with the project under way. By the time the veining stage is reached it is a bit late to change your mind on the timber, so practise veining on a spare piece of the same timber before veining the project.

Using a sample of the timber used for Project 1, draw up a few leaves. Experiment with drawing different styles of veins on them to see what they look like, keeping in mind that it is best not to get too carried away the first time. Try to keep the veins as natural as possible, with as few stiff, straight lines as can be managed (though some plants do have straight veins).

Here are some different methods of leaf veining. I recommended that you try all of them and then choose the one that works best with the timber you are using.

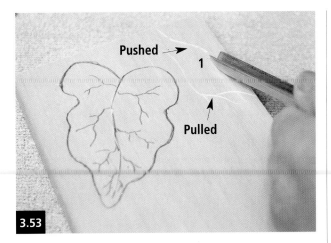

3.53

1 USING THE V-TOOL

3.53 The V-tool, as its name suggests, cuts a V-shaped groove in the timber. Where a smaller V is needed, a smaller size of V-tool can be used, or you can improvise somehow.

If you use the V-tool by drawing it towards your body, it 'dents' the wood (as opposed to cutting it, as it does when pushed). The value of this is that the tool is less likely to stick and tear; the disadvantage is that it is hard to see where you are going, and it only works in softwood.

3.54

2 USING THE CARVING KNIFE

3.54 If extremely fine lines are required, then scoring with the knife is a handy technique to use. Care must be taken that the knife does not dig in and leave ugly marks. It can also be hard to get fluid curves using the knife – corners can look stiff and jointed like stick-figure drawings.

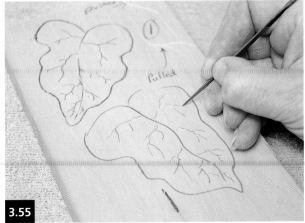

3.55

3 USING AN IMPROVISED TOOL

3.55 If the veins are not to be heavily indented, scoring with a sharp nail or similar is very simple. In this photo a slender spike is being used: it is easy to control and you can see where it's heading. When scoring veins it is always easier to work towards the body, not away from it – unless a V-tool or gouge is being used.

4 THE RAISED METHOD

Leaving the veins standing above the height of the surrounding wood is complex and time-consuming; there are two ways to achieve it.

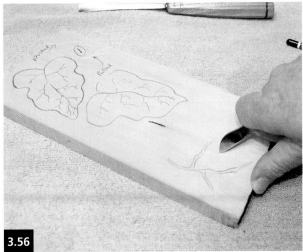

3.56

3.56 *Method A* Pencil in double lines to show the veins and cut down alongside with the knife. For clarity, the photograph shows the knife hold being demonstrated on waste wood.

3.57

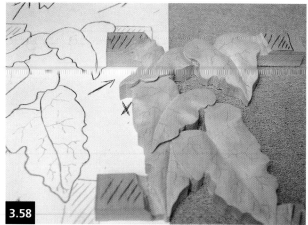

3.58

3.57 Cut away the timber either side of the lines to leave the vein raised, then sand.

Method B Lightly mark with chalk where the veins are required, lay a clean piece of rounded steel or other metal along the line of the vein and tap with a small hammer so the wood is indented. The wood is then pared back level, basted with warm water and left to dry. The water will swell the wood that was pushed down and raise it above the now lowered surrounding timber; then sand to finish. This is a difficult and tedious process that is often used when carving the human body, if veins need to be shown. It is not recommended for these projects.

You need to decide:
• what style of veining suits the project
• what style of veining best suits the timber you are using
• what style of veining you feel most confident of achieving on this timber.

3.58 For this project in jelutong I recommend method 3 as the simplest and most effective. Draw veins on the paper design, then lightly pencil them onto the workpiece. The photograph shows the leaves with the veins completed using method 3.

3.59

3.59 When veining has been achieved, rub over lightly with 400-grit or similar sandpaper to remove any rough edges from the veins.

Finishing the surface

Before proceeding further it is essential to finish the face of the carving. Once the undercutting is completed the whole thing will become more fragile to handle, which is a good reason to finish it now.

3.60

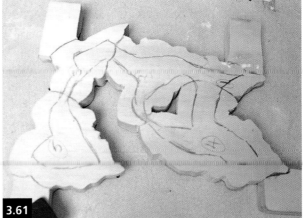

3.61

3.60 Using a clean paintbrush, brush the entire carved surfaces over with hot tap water. Do not soak or immerse the carving, as this may cause cracking or splitting. Allow it to dry overnight.

When the timber is dry, rub over the whole face with no. 0000 or 000 steel wool. The hot water will raise the grain, making the fibres stand up, and rubbing with steel wool will remove them, leaving a fine finish. Brush over with a clean, dry paintbrush to remove loose particles.

Undercutting the edges

The purpose here is not to remove all the timber from the back of the leaves, but just enough to make them interesting. Enough wood must be left untouched to ensure that there will be plenty of strength to fix the front to the backing board later. It is important to realize that the aim is a cut that will complement what has been done so far, not just remove wood.

Turn the design over and pencil on the tabs where the edges of the leaves meet, but do not cut them yet. They will not be cut until much later, as the strength is needed to hold the design while it is being worked on. The value of the tabs is now evident, as they hold the workpiece safely while we carve the back, without any damage to the front of the carving.

3.61 Number the leaves on the back for identification, as on the front. Make a pencil mark about 1/2in (12mm) in from the edges all around the design. It is important that a 'bridge' be left intact between the leaves to hold the design together.

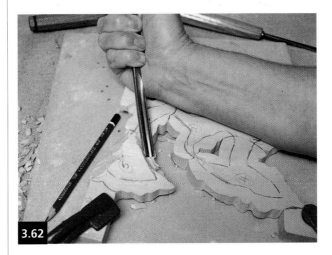

3.62

3.62 A 9/10 gouge is here being used to make a hollow cut or cove on the edge of leaf 5. This is the opposite of the profile which has been carved on the face of the leaf, and using this shape on the undercut will make the leaf edge very prominent.

At the top of leaf 5 (near the pencil) the V-tool has been used to open the centre, and the fishtail used on the tips.

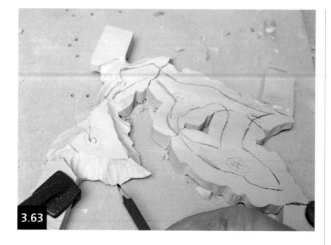

3.63

3.65

3.63 Here the pencil is pointing to where the back of the leaf has been shaped to follow the front contour. It has a wavy look to match the front. The 9/10 gouge was used for this, cutting downwards carefully. Take particular notice of the tab: part of it has been cut away, but lots of timber has been left for strength.

3.65 Tight cuts can be made either with the 8/7 gouge, as shown here, or by using the V-tool.

3.64

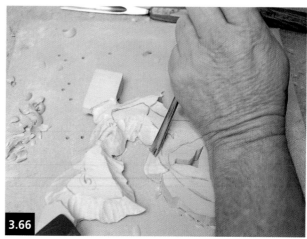

3.66

3.64 The 9/10 gouge has been used again on the outer edges of leaf 3; it can also be seen that plenty of wood has been left on the tab. The cut is made to follow the shape of the leaf by using the fishtail to round it; the pencil points to an area where this can be seen clearly.

3.66 The top of leaf 2 is rounded with the fishtail, so as to keep adequate strength while cutting back into leaf 3. If a cove cut were made here, it would result in a hole being cut in the leaf.

3.67 Work along leaf 4, alternating the 9/10 and the fishtail as needed to conform to the shape. Take care when approaching the tip of leaf 1.

3.70 Turn the design and continue to cut away waste. Note the steep angle at which the gouge has to be used in tight areas.

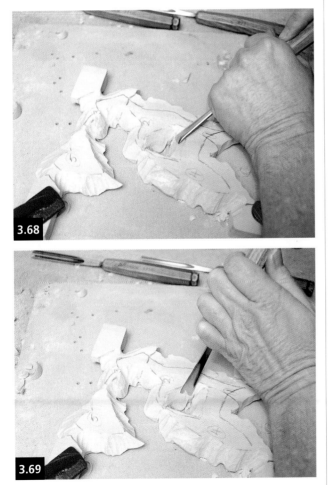

3.71 Elsewhere, a longer bevel is produced by cutting from further back, with the gouge held at a shallower angle.

3.68 and 3.69 These two photographs show the centre being shaped and cut back with the fishtail.

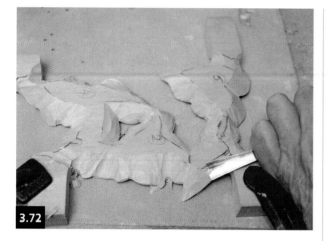

3.72

3.72 Take care not to remove the tip of the leaf when approaching it with the fishtail.

3.74

Preparing to mount the carving

3.74 Carefully and slowly cut off the tab on leaf no. 3, using either gouge and cutting the timber away a little at a time from the back.

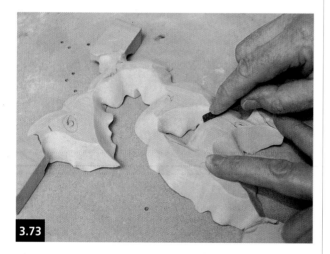

3.73

3.73 Sand all the cut edges, working through the grades of sandpaper starting with the coarsest. Take care not to lean heavily on the fragile edges; support the tips with your fingers as required, and work along entire surfaces.

3.75

3.75 Turn the work face up to cut the edge neatly with the fishtail, then sand.

3.76

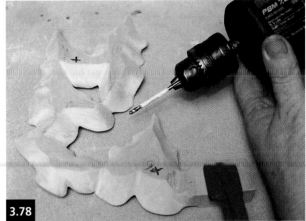

3.78

3.76 Working from the front, cut away the tab on leaf no. 1, taking small cuts with the 8/7 gouge; then turn over to tidy up and sand.

3.78 Use your fingers to feel for the thickest part of leaves 5 and 4, and mark these with an X in pencil. Turn the design face down and hold by the remaining tab.

A piece of masking tape has been wound on the 1/8in (3mm) drill to act as a depth gauge. This will show the depth as you drill, so the bit does not go too deep and come out on the face. Drill one hole at each place marked; these will be for the dowels to mount the carving on its backing board.

Pressing gently to hold the design in place, slowly and carefully cut away the last remaining tab and then sand.

Using hot clean water and a clean brush, wet the undercuts to raise the grain and allow to dry. When dry, rub lightly with 0000 or 000 steel wool and dust off any debris with a brush. Inspect the project carefully: if there are marks or pick-outs on the face, the time to fix them is now. When the timber is oiled, any marks will show up even more than they do at the moment.

3.77

3.77 Holding the design by the tab on leaf 5, cut away the tab from leaf 4 and sand. Take care not to run the chisel into the clamp.

3.79 Using the two drills that were used earlier, carefully make a few holes in the face to represent bug holes (this is optional). A small nail can be used for the tiny holes. Clean up with rolled sandpaper. Once coloured, these marks will look very natural.

The backing board
The wood being used is the piece of rosewood that was cut on the bandsaw earlier (see page 16); we will finish it with a bevelled edge.

3.80 Clamp the timber firmly to the bench, but slide a piece of leather or cardboard under the clamp so as not to mark or dent the surface of the timber.

A non-skid mat underneath also helps to keep it in place on the bench and stop it moving.

Sand the back of the board, the face and the outer edges, using sandpaper wrapped around a block of wood or a cork block. Take care to keep the edges square and flat, and work through the grades of sandpaper until a smooth finish has been achieved. Move the clamp as necessary to access the whole of the board.

Measure on the surface 1/2in (12mm) all around the face of the board and 1/4in (6mm) down the sides, and mark clearly as shown. This is the area that will be bevelled: the front corner is what will be removed.

3.81 Using the fishtail chisel and holding it at the angle shown, cut down towards the lower pencil line. Slowly work along the outer edge of the board, ensuring that all cuts are kept within the waste section. Do not worry that the surface of the bevel is not completely flat, as the bastard file will be used to level it out.

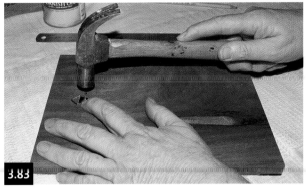

3.82

3.82 Hold the file as shown and slowly push it at the same angle as the bevelled edge. The angle here is most important: if the hand is either too high or too low, the face of the bevel will be altered. The pencil lines are there to be used as a guide, so keep an eye on them.

The use of the file makes it far simpler to get a nice flat surface than trying to do it with a chisel, and it is less likely that the edges will break or splinter. If the file gets clogged with splinters of wood, use a wire brush to clean it.

If you have a hand plane, you could use this instead to bevel the edges.

When all the edges have been levelled, wrap sandpaper around the file to keep it nice and flat and sand the bevel. Repeat using the required number of grades of paper until a fine finish has been reached.

Brush over the entire backing board with hot tap water and a clean brush, allow to dry, and sand with 0000 or 000 steel wool.

Finishing

Refer to Chapter 8 for the method of staining (if required) and oiling. In this case the rosewood backing did not need staining, but has been oiled and rubbed back twice with steel wool before a last wipe over with a cloth lightly moistened with Danish oil. It has been allowed to dry and harden.

3.83 Place the backing face down on a mat or towel so as not to damage the face. Measure and mark on the centre line of the board 1¹/₂in (38mm) down from the top edge; this is where the hanger will be fixed. If the hanger is left until after the carving has been attached, there is a risk of damaging the carving, so it is easier to do it now.

As this total project is not heavy one, a small flap hanger will be sufficient to hold it. Place the flap on the centre mark and with a small hammer tap in the pins provided with the flap.

Once the front section has been carved, stained, oiled, and is dry, it can be attached to the back with dowels and glue.

3.84

Attaching the carving to the backing board

3.84 Place the carved front piece face down on cloth so as not to scratch the polish. Use tracing paper to make a template of the back area. Transfer this to white paper and lay the template on the back of the carving, using wooden meat skewers (kebab sticks) to locate the dowel holes.

(Note that the template differs in shape from the carving because parts of it have been cut away to enable masking tape to be placed to hold it to the back of the carving.)

3.86

3.86 Turn the paper again and locate it back onto the carving, matching up the dowel holes with the skewers as before. You may need to tear away some of the paper, just enough to stick on small strips of tape to hold the template in place when the skewers are removed.

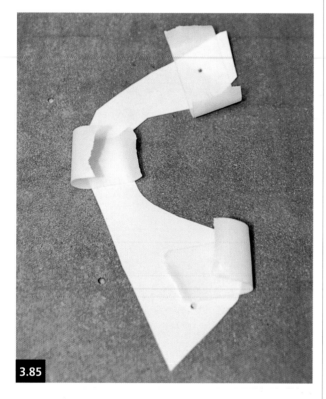

3.85

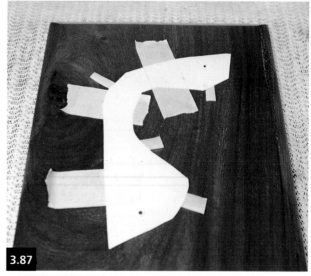

3.87

3.85 Remove the skewers and turn the paper over onto a board. Lay strips of masking tape across the template, with plenty of overhang on each side dangling free.

3.87 Carefully remove the skewers and gently place the carving onto the backing board in what will be its permanent position. Press the larger pieces of masking tape to the backing board and hold them firmly down while the carving is being removed. The template is now in position for the drilling of the corresponding dowel holes.

3.88

3.88 Using the ⅛in (3mm) drill, with masking tape as before for a depth gauge, drill through the paper where the holes are. Remove the template from the backing board and blow out any dust or shavings.

Cut lengths of skewer to use as dowels, equal to the depth of the hole in the backing plus the depth of the hole in the carving, or fractionally less. Kebab sticks are made of bamboo and are exceptionally strong and flexible, which is ideal for small projects such as this that have almost no weight.

Sand the reverse of the carving where glue will be applied. Take care that the edges do not get damaged – it is best to keep the sanding in from the edges, as its purpose is only to give the glue a grip.

Rub a small area around the dowel holes on the backing board for the glue to grip; take care not to go too far, or it will show.

Use good-quality glue: my preference is for two-part epoxy wood glue, but any good wood glue will do. (Instant glue will not allow enough time to

get things lined up.) Make sure that the dowel holes have glue pushed into them with a piece of skewer; the dowels should squeeze the glue from the holes when they are inserted. The holes are slightly bigger than the actual dowels, which will allow plenty of glue to grip all surfaces and let any air escape.

Spread the glue on the back of the carving, making sure that the whole of the contact surface is covered. Wipe any glue from the edges with a clean cloth, and align the dowels in the carving with the holes in the backing board. Press firmly but carefully.

Check to make sure that glue has not oozed out around the design. If this has happened, remove the carving, wipe off the excess and refit.

3.89

3.89 Place a clean cotton cloth on top of the carving and leave a weight on it for 24 hours; a small bag of sand works well.

4 Flower and leaf panel

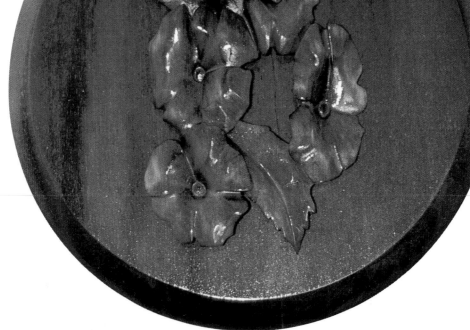

TIMBER

Carving: jelutong, 8 x 9in (203 x 229mm)

  x 1/2in (12mm) thick

Backing: jelutong, 10in (254mm) diameter

  x 1/2in (12mm) thick

Preparation

Trace the design onto your chosen timber (jelutong in my case), including the tabs. Take care to position the design so that the grain is running in the required direction; watch out for any faults in the plank. Ensure that the waste timber around the design is again marked WXYZ so that test cuts for grain direction can be made.

Drill out the tight corners and cut out the pattern ready for working as before, test the grain direction and mark this with arrows on the pattern (see pages 16–19). Place the spare pattern, with arrows marked on it, where it can be seen while working. Number the leaves and flowers as in the pattern.

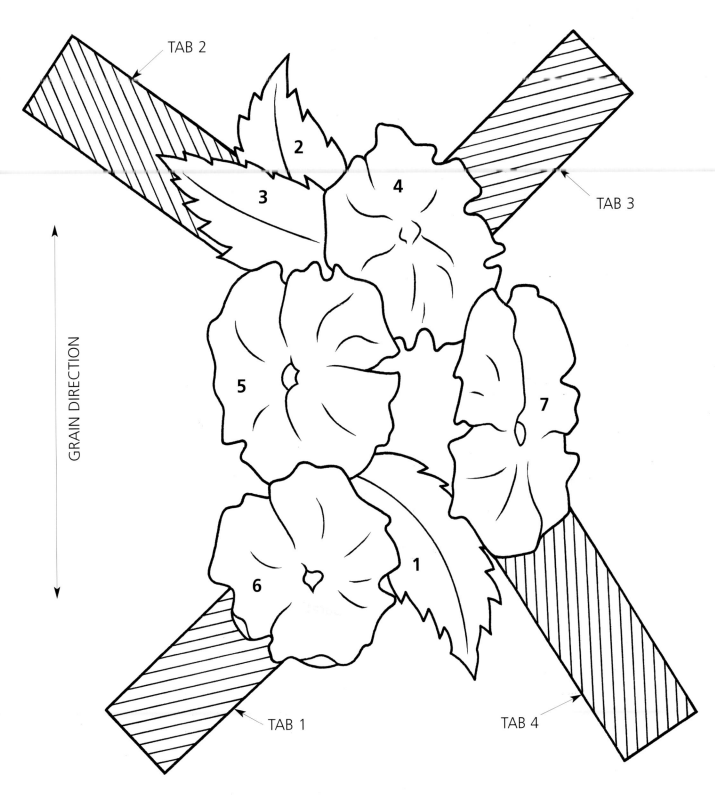

TAB 2

TAB 3

GRAIN DIRECTION

2

3

4

5

7

6

1

TAB 1

TAB 4

*To make this drawing
full size, enlarge on a
photocopier to 112%*

Modelling and carving leaf no. 1

Make the model of leaf 1 in the same manner as before, by flattening the material between boards and then cutting round the profile with a knife (see page 20).

Timber Using the 5/3 and 3/5 gouges, stab-cut downwards between elements 1 and 6, 1 and 5, 1 and 7.

4.1

4.1 ***Clay*** As leaf 1 is the lowest of the group, it will need to have its thickness reduced so that it lies below the flowers. Remove enough clay to reduce the thickness of the model by 1/4in (6mm) over its entire surface. Cut a V out of the centre line of the clay and lower both of the ends.

Timber Use the fishtail to lower the level of the wood; it does not have to be flat. Cut the centre line using the knife, lower both ends of the leaf with the fishtail and cut out a V each side of the centre line.

Leaf no. 2

Turn the design around and stab-cut between leaves 2 and 3.

4.2

4.2 ***Clay*** Lower the height of the clay as for the first leaf, then lower the left side (next to flower no. 4) to give it a slope. Remove a V from the centre.

Timber Reduce the thickness and lower the left side as for the model, using the fishtail, and cut a V out of the centre.

4.3

Leaf no. 3

4.3 ***Clay*** Lower the rear (wide) end of the leaf and make a central V-cut.

Timber With 5/3 and 3/5 gouges, cut between 3 and 4, then 3 and 5; turn the chisel as needed to get into tight corners.

Do not cut leaf 3 where it lies on the tab; leave this area and lower only the rest of the leaf to make it slope down towards flower 4. Cut the central V in leaf 3 in the same manner as before, using either the V-tool or the fishtail.

Flower no. 4

This is a good time to discuss the shape of the flowers that are about to be carved. They are an 'open' type similar to pansy, hibiscus and brunfelsia, and allow a lot of leeway in interpretation. It is helpful to have a mental picture of similar flowers to work from – or it may be possible to pick one from the garden.

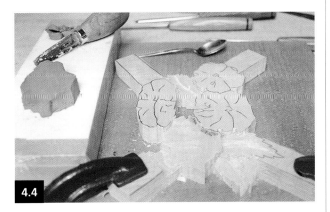

4.4 Use the 5/3 and 3/5 gouges to separate 4 from 5 and 7 by stab-cutting downwards. Cut a trench 1/4in (6mm) deep in the tab where it touches flower 4, and stab-cut the edges of 4 to conform to the contour.

Clay and timber Lower the entire outer edge of the flower to make it slope down to the tab.

4.5 **Clay** Use the knife to bevel off all the edges, and then use a kebab skewer to draw the centre of the flower.

Timber Use the fishtail to chamfer all the edges of the flower, and mark the centre with pencil.

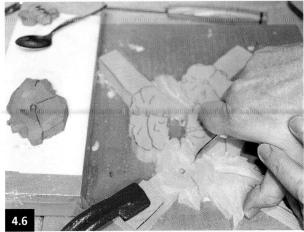

4.6 **Clay** Use a teaspoon to gouge out the centre, and a kebab stick to mark in the petals.

Timber Using the 9/10 gouge, cut towards the middle, starting 1/2in (12mm) from the centre and working clockwise. Soften the edges of the hole with the fishtail. Use the carving knife to cut petal lines, angling the blade *only slightly* so that we will have a small undercut when the petals are shaped.

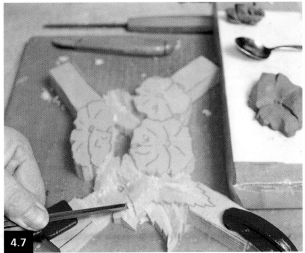

4.7 **Clay** Decide which edge of the petal is to be higher than its neighbour; removing clay from only one side creates 'lift'.

Timber Cut towards the petal line with the 3/5 gouge to separate the edges. Alternate the levels: one side up, and one down.

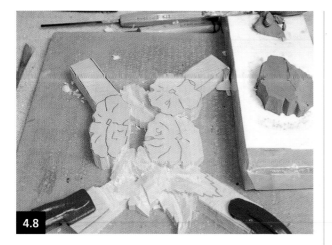
4.8

Flower no. 5

4.8 *Clay* Draw in the centre and lower the right side of the flower.

Timber Stab-cut between 5 and 6, then use the fishtail to lower the right side.

4.10

4.10 *Clay* Use a spoon to gouge out the centre, then draw petals and centre with the kebab skewer. Lower the clay at the petal edges as for the previous flower, to show difference in levels. Use a teaspoon handle to scoop out dips in the outer petals.

Timber Use the 9/10 and the 8/7 to gouge out the central area, working in the same manner as with the first flower. Mark the petals first with a pencil, then cut them in with the carving knife. Using the 3/5, cut towards the petal edges, alternating the levels as with the previous flower. Use the 8/7 gouge to cut grooves in the outer edges of the petals; the pencil in the photograph is pointing to these.

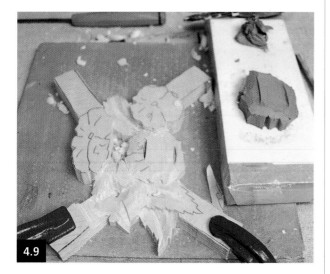
4.9

4.9 *Clay* Divide the width of the flower into thirds, then bevel all around the outside of the flower.

Timber Mark in the same way, using the fishtail to remove the outer edges.

4.11

Flower no. 6

4.11 Stab-cut the outer edge of the design, then cut a trench in the tab down to half the thickness of the timber.

4.12 **Clay** Make a mark one third of the way across the flower, and use the knife to cut away the clay on the left side.

Timber Mark in the same place as on the clay, and use the fishtail to lower from the pencil mark almost to the depth of the cut in the trench. The cut should be angled down towards the trench, which will tip the flower in that direction.

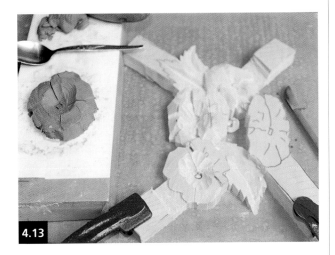

4.13 **Clay** Use the spoon to gouge out the centre, then draw in the petal lines with the kebab stick.

Timber Using either the 8/7 or the 9/10, gouge out the central area as with the other flowers. Use the knife to cut in the petal lines, then redraw the centre and cut.

4.14 **Clay** Separate the petals by scraping clay from one side, then use the spoon to gouge dips in the outer edges of the flower.

Timber Use the 3/5 to lower one side of the petal as before, then the 8/7 to gouge dips in the outer edges (marked in pencil) to create ripples.

Flower no. 7

4.15 **Timber** Stab-cut along the outline where the tab touches, then cut a trench in the tab to half the thickness of the timber.

Clay Use the knife to remove a slice from left edge of the model.

Timber Use the fishtail to remove wood from the corresponding area.

4.16

4.18

4.16 ***Clay*** Mark the centre, then remove a slice of clay from the right side of the central mark almost down to the board (the wedge removed can be seen at the top of the photograph).
Timber Pencil in the centre, then use the fishtail to lower the entire right side to within ⅛in (3mm) of the backing board.

4.18 ***Clay*** Cut one side of the petal to lower it, scoop out the outer petals and recut the centre.
Timber Lower one side of the petal with the 3/5 as before to create separation, then use the 8/7 gouge to create dips in the outer petals. Recut the centre.

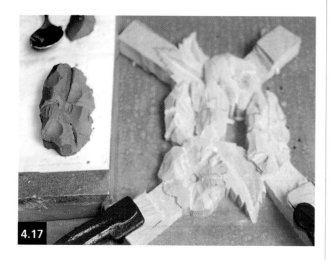

4.17

4.19

4.17 ***Clay*** Use the spoon to scoop out the centre. Mark the petal lines.
Timber Use either of the gouges to scoop out the centre. Cut the petal lines with the knife.

Sanding and undercutting
4.19 Undercut the petals of flowers 6 and 7 where they overlap the other flowers and leaves in the same way as the first project (see pages 28–30), then work through the grades of sandpaper until a fine finish has been achieved.

4.20 Undercut in the same manner where flower 6 overhangs flower 5, and sand all over.

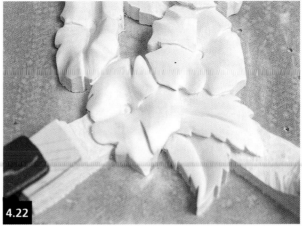

4.22 Take care when undercutting between leaves 2 and 3 so as not to lose the fine serrated edges of leaf 3; sand all.

4.21 Undercut where flowers 7 and 5 overhang no. 4, and sand to finish.

Carefully stab-cut along leaf 3 where it lies on the tab, and lower the tab to half its thickness. Undercut where flower 5 overhangs, and sand all over.

4.23 Undercut where 5, 6 and 7 overhang leaf 1, and sand all.

Decide what style of veining is suitable (see pages 30–2) and vein all three leaves, then sand lightly with 400 grit. Wet the timber as previously described, allow to dry, then rub with steel wool and remove the dust.

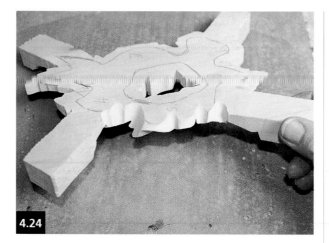

4.24

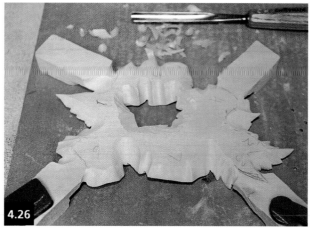

4.26

Undercutting the edges

4.24 Lightly pencil on the back the area to be undercut, as we did with the first project (page 33). Make sure that the bridges between the flowers and leaves are strong enough to hold the design together.

Before cutting any material, pay attention to what has happened to the front of the wood. If the flower or leaf on the front is lying close to the backing (as flower 5 is), then the undercut area will be small. As before, the size and shape of the undercut must be relevant to the shape of the front of the carving.

4.26 Without removing the tabs, work around the entire outer edge, turning the design for easy access as required. Sand each section as it is completed.

4.25

4.27

4.25 Clamp the design to the work bench and, using whichever gouge or chisel suits the undercut, carve the area between the tabs. Work only a small section at a time, then sand. Do not cut the tabs away yet.

4.27 Using thumb and finger, feel for the thickest parts of the design and mark three places (the spacing between them need not be exactly equal) for the dowels. Place tape on the drill for a depth gauge, and drill each hole for the dowels at the marked spots, as for the first project.

Clamping firmly as shown, carefully and using small cuts remove the tab from leaf 3, clean up the edge and sand.

4.28

4.29

4.28 Move across and do the same to the tab at flower 6. Turn the design, and carefully remove part of the tabs on flowers 7 and 4, but do not cut either of these right through. Work slowly between these two tabs, cutting small slivers of each one in turn until they are free. Tidy the edges and sand.

Wet all the undercuts; allow them to dry, then sand.

The backing board

The jelutong for the backing board has already been planed and sanded.

The size of the circle for the backing is 10in (254mm). This can be marked with a compass or protractor, or by using a dinner plate or a large tin – anything to give the size required.

If a bandsaw is available, cut the timber carefully, staying outside the marked line. A circle can be cut effectively using a handsaw by making lots of small segmented cuts around the outside; the edges are then straightened up with the bastard file.

4.29 Place a piece of leather or cardboard and a small block of waste under the clamp to protect the surface from being damaged or crushed, moving it as required as you work.

Using the bastard file and keeping it upright to the timber, clean off the saw marks all around the edge of the circle.

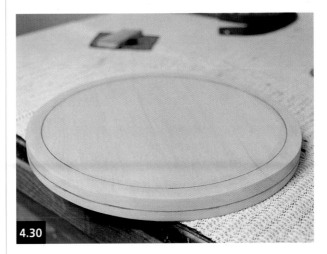

4.30

4.30 Clearly mark ¹⁄₈in (3mm) from the back edge and ¹⁄₂in (12mm) from the edge of the top face: this is the section to be removed.

4.31

4.31 Using the fishtail chisel in the same manner as for the first project, bevel the edge. Work small sections at a time, moving the timber and the clamp as you work your way around the circle.

4.32

4.32 Use the bastard file to level the surface of the angle, then sand.

4.33

4.33 The carving is laid on the backing. Because of its paleness I decided to stain the whole project as described on pages 96–7.

Fix a flap hanger 1¹/₂in (38mm) from the top of the backing board. Place the board face down on cloth for this operation, taking care that the grain is vertical when the board hangs straight.

4.34

Fixing the carving to the backing

4.34 Three dowel holes have already been made in the carving. Make a template and locate the holes as for the first project (pages 39–40).

4.35

4.35 Place masking tape in position and lay the carving face up in the required position on the backing. Press the tape firmly to the backing to hold the template, and gently remove the carving, leaving the template behind.

The guide for the dowel holes can be seen clearly in the template. Drill them as before, then cut three dowels from a kebab stick. Glue the carving to the backing, checking that the glue has not oozed out from behind the design. Cover with a cloth and place a suitable weight on it for 24 hours.

5 Lop-eared rabbit

TIMBER

Carving: Pacific mahogany, 8 x 11in
(203 x 280mm) x 2in (50mm) thick

Backing: colonial pine, 10³/4 x 13in
(273 x 330mm) x ¹/2in (12mm) thick

You will find that Pacific mahogany has a very different feel from the previously used jelutong. It is a much denser timber, and cuts more cleanly; this will allow us to leave some of the surfaces with an unsanded 'chisel' finish, and also to obtain a higher finish on the areas we do sand. Although this wood requires a little more effort, it is not difficult to cut. I would recommend it to a carver of any level of expertise.

'Colonial pine' is a colloquial name for Australian kauri. This timber cuts cleanly and is very strong. Care needs to be taken when working against the grain, as the chisel can tend to 'dig in' and cause splitting or lifting of fibres.

This is the kind of project where making a clay model is most helpful. Now that you have the feel of the chisels and have gained some confidence in working with the clay, it is time to move on. By making a full model of the project first, any problems with perspective and depth can be solved quickly and simply. The model allows you to become familiar with the shape of the subject without ruining the timber.

The subject is an English lop with exceptionally long ears. Besides learning how to handle the perspective, there is a variety of textures to practise with. The crate that the rabbit is on will be chisel-finished, and the straw also will be left unsanded. The bunny will be sanded to a smooth finish which will contrast well with the other textures.

Please take note that where I refer to the 'left side' I mean *your* left as you are looking at the design, not the left side of the rabbit. This applies throughout the book.

As before, test offcuts on this and all future projects before starting work.

The clay model

The basic principle of making a working model is the same as for those you have done previously – only the size is different. Ensure that the finished model is the same thickness as the timber you intend to use for the carving; this will be crucial when we start measuring from the model.

Lay heavy plastic on a piece of chipboard and tape it in place. Build up the thickness of clay as you did for the smaller models; the only difference here is that you will require more clay. Use offcuts of the carving timber to test the thickness (by placing a piece either side as we did before), and bash it flat until it reaches the same thickness as the timber you are about to carve.

5.1

5.1 Lay the cut-out design on top of the clay block and cut away the excess from around it as we did for the others. Leave the pattern on the clay and use a sharp nail or skewer to prick along the inner lines of the drawing, so that the dots will be left when the paper design is removed.

5.2

5.2 Carefully remove the design and use the kebab stick to join up the dots, leaving clearly drawn lines on the clay.

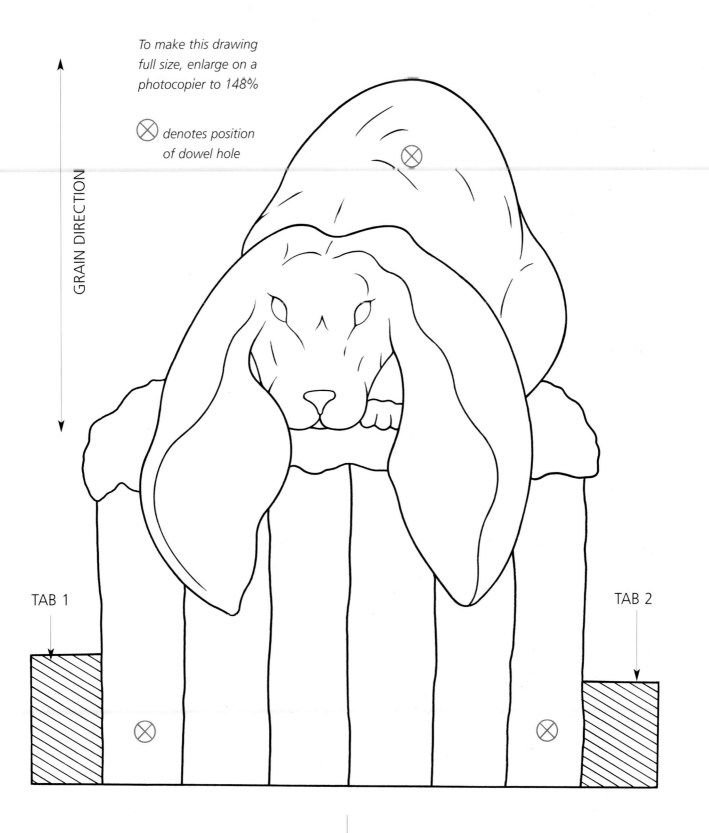

GRAIN DIRECTION

To make this drawing
full size, enlarge on a
photocopier to 148%

⊗ denotes position
of dowel hole

TAB 1

TAB 2

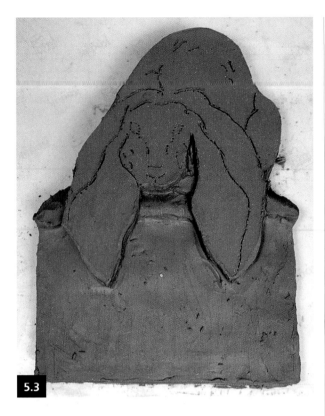

5.3

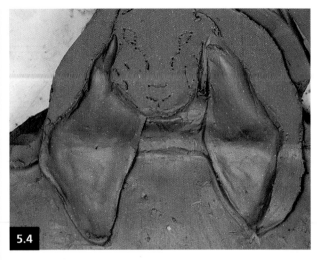

5.4

5.4 The inside of the left ear has been hollowed by scraping with a spoon and smoothing over with the fingers; the flat part where it hangs over the crate has been left at ¼in (6mm) thick. Notice that it has been left quite thick along the line of the straw at the top of the crate: this will give the impression of the thin ear being distorted by the straw. The outer left edge of the ear is left higher to allow for the curve. The deeper hollow where it is level with the eye has been cut to ½in (12mm) depth.

Do the same with the right ear, leaving a curve in the ear with the inner edge slightly higher.

5.3 Mark a line in the clay ¾in (18mm) down around the outside edges of the crate. Use a spoon or a blunt knife to lower the clay to this depth all the way to the edge of the ears. The ears are now standing above the level of the crate, and the straw is hanging over.

Scrape the straw back away from the edge of the ears to leave the line clear, and clean the clay from under the rabbit's chin and along the inside of the right ear. Do not worry about the detail of the right foot at this stage.

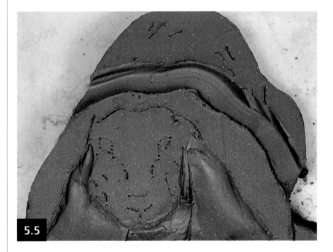

5.5

5.5 To separate the line of the ears and head from the body, cut a ½in (12mm) trench around the line at the back of the ears into the body and hind leg. This allows access to the curve of the ears, and gives a clear line to mark the body.

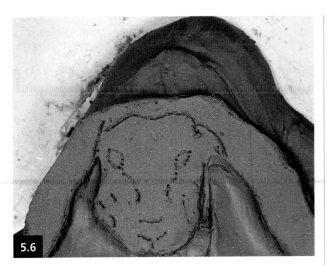

5.6 Shape the rabbit's back by sloping the clay sharply to the hump of the shoulders and then rounding it to the back wall for the bulge of the belly and the back. The rear leg is cut back to an elongated oval with a sharp hollow between it and the body. The whole shape of the body has to be fitted into this area from behind the head, or else there will not be enough room in the material for the head itself.

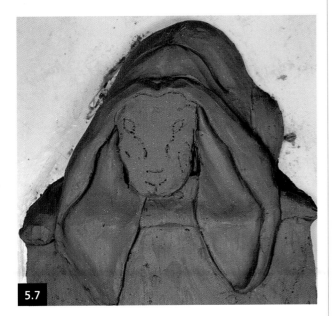

5.7 The sharp square edges are removed from the outer edges of the ears, rounding them and giving them fullness. The flat section on the top of the head has been sloped by removing the front corner and flattening it across the brow.

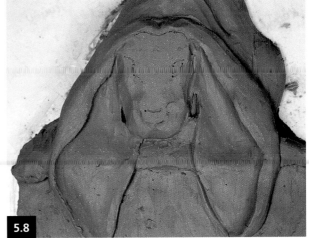

5.8 Remove ⅛in (3mm) of clay from the inner edges of the ears to make them curl or flop inwards a little. The bridge of the nose is the closest part of the head, so all the rest must be shaped back or away from this point and made to fit to the ears.

Shape the fullness of the area round the mouth. Slope from where the ears join down along the sides of the face, working the hollow below the eyes.

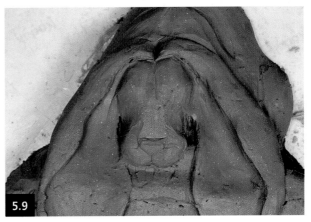

5.9 Cut a V in the centre of the head to mark the depth of the skull, then take a wedge from the ear line and the top of the brow to round the head. Scrape a groove down to the centre point between the eyes, slope the clay away from this point and round it off.

From above the pad of the nose, cut a small slice and scrape the clay up to the bridge to leave a hump or 'Roman' look. Deepen the hollow along the sides of the central ridge of the face.

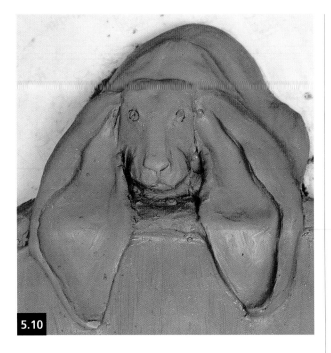

5.10

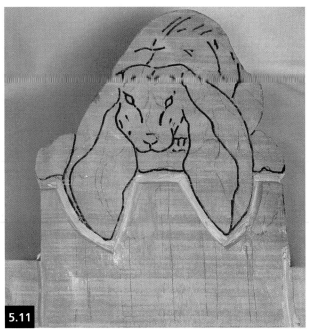

5.11

5.10 With the skewer, mark in the position of the eyes and the mouth. Cut in where the heavy muscle of the ears fits in at the top and side of the head, remove some of the clay from the top flat part of the skull, and smooth it with the fingers.

Use the handle of the teaspoon to scrape some clay from the mouth/chin area and from the side of the nostrils, reducing the full part of the cheeks.

Carving

Bandsaw the profile of the rabbit with the two tabs intact. Turn it over and drill the three 1/4in (6mm) holes, 1/2in (12mm) deep, marked on the drawing; these will be used later to dowel the bunny to the backing. Make a template of the dowel holes, ready for attaching him to the backing.

· Please note that in the following photographs clamps have been removed for clarity.

5.11 Holding the work by the tabs, mark a line 5/8in (15mm) down around the outside of the crate; this is the level to which the surface of the crate needs to be reduced.

With the V-tool or either of the gouges, cut a trench outside the line of the ears and the straw into the timber of the crate. This trench does not have to be tidy or fussy; it is to stop the chisels running into the ears and to stop the timber splitting while we are removing waste from the crate. Cut a line also between the tabs and the crate, for the same reason.

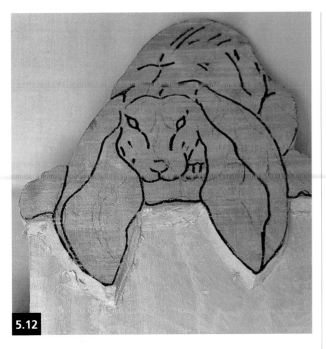

5.12

5.13

5.12 Use the 9/10 or the fishtail to lower the level of the crate to the bottom of the trench. Recut the trench and again lower the level of the box until the pencil line has almost been reached; then finish by working lightly over with the fishtail to remove the worst of the humps.

Note that the right ear has had its edges tidied by stab-cutting gently around the design; repeat along the edge of the straw and the left ear. Do not tap with the mallet when stab-cutting – push the chisel gently but firmly with the hand only, so as not to mark the lower level. Choose the chisel that matches the curve you are cutting.

5.13 Before any further shaping can be started, you must decide what type of finish will be used. I have chosen to give the crate a tooled finish; this means that it will not be sanded, but left as is after the chisel has been used.

Lightly redraw the planks on the front of the crate as a guide, deciding on their width and number. Working each board separately, so that chisel marks do not cross from one board to the next, will prevent the crate looking like one large slab.

Use the 8/7 to work from the bottom of the crate up towards the rabbit in short strokes – or reverse the direction if you find this gives a cleaner cut. By varying the length of the cuts – some short, some long – you can give a convincingly rough, uneven look to the boards. Some alteration in the depth of the cuts can also be used, but take care not to snap the timber off.

When the ears are reached, just leave the last cut undone; this will be finished when we undercut them much later.

Separation of the boards is achieved by dragging the carving knife down firmly along the pencil lines; repeating the cut on the same mark with the blade very slightly angled will leave the tiniest sliver to be picked out. Wavy lines or odd gaps only serve to make it more interesting, so don't wrestle to get it too even.

Holes have been marked for nails. This can be done by tapping a nail punch into the timber, or by cutting the tip from a 2in (50mm) nail and tapping it gently with a small tack hammer where needed. The overhanging straw hides the top row of nails.

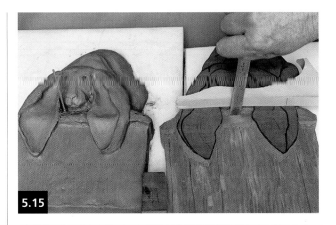

5.15

5.15 Test the depth of the clay representing the straw in front of the bunny's chin. By laying a flat offcut on the uncut surface, the depth can be repeatedly checked as the straw is cut back. Repeat this procedure to cut back the straw either side of the ears, and roughly shape under the face.

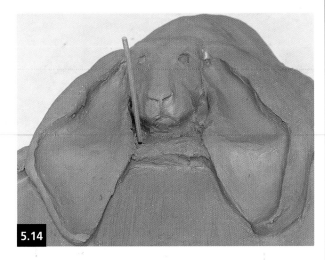

5.14

5.14 Carefully stab-cut around the lines of the ears and face, using the carving knife or whichever chisel fits the curves.

From here on is where our model proves its worth. You can push a kebab skewer all the way through the clay to the backing board and mark the depth of the clay on it, as shown. Alternatively, mark the depth with your thumbnail and then measure the length of the skewer when it is withdrawn. This measurement gives us the required depth needed at that place on the timber – all we have to do is keep testing the depth as we work around the profile. Depths must be tested often and related to the timber. So as not to get lost when working, it is best to work small areas at a time.

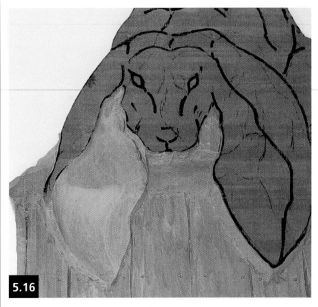

5.16

5.16 Working from the tip of the left ear, test the depths in the clay and cut the timber back to match, making sure that the ridge is kept where the ear hangs over the protruding straw. Showing the contour of the surface underneath it gives the impression that the ear is very thin and delicate – which it is.

Use the 9/10 to remove larger amounts of timber and the fishtail to level the surface. When working along the inner line of the ear, use either gouge and cut parallel to the line; this will leave a slight curve on the lower level. Measure frequently and compare with the clay model.

For tight curves use the 8/7. Do not try to finish the top inside of the ear next to face now – this will be done when the face is profiled.

Sand the ear with 180 or 240 grit to give a clearer view of the work, rolling the paper for the curves. Final sanding will be done at a later time.

5.18 Sand the right ear, then cut a trench behind the head and ears as we did in the clay. Remove the bulk of the waste from the rabbit's back with the 9/10, and finish off with the fishtail.

Use the 9/10 for the depression behind the shoulder blades, and the 8/7 for the tight curve behind the head and between the shoulders at the neck. The ridge of the backbone is left prominent.

Cut the deeper groove where the hind leg joins the body, and sand the back all over with 180 or 240 grit.

5.17 Reduce the waste with the 3/5 next to the right cheek between head and ear.

The photograph shows the right ear carved but not sanded. Use the same method of testing the clay first and then cutting to match. No undercutting of the ears will be undertaken yet.

From here on it will be assumed that the clay is tested for depth before cutting the timber, even though it is not stated every time.

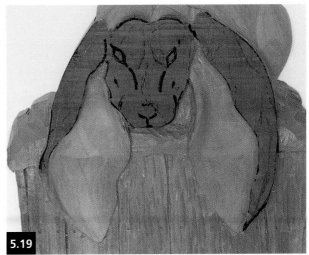

5.19 Use the fishtail to cut in at the top of the ears as shown, and slope the flat part of the head to match the model, keeping the central depression. A blue pencil mark has been drawn to show where the rounding of the back of the ears will begin.

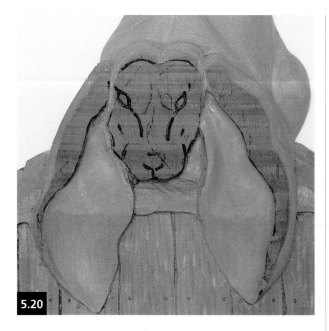

5.20

5.20 Use the fishtail to round the back of the ears to the blue pencil mark, checking the contours against the model. With the V-tool, cut a groove between the ears and the top of the head, rounding the top of the head to make it fit if needed. Notice that at the top and back of the ears the V has been cut a little sharper; use the 3/5 to do this, as it helps to give more depth.

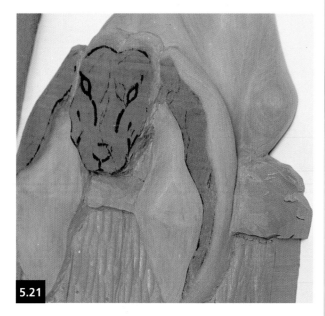

5.21

5.21 Now that the shape of the ears has been set, the back of the ears and the area behind them can be worked. Starting at the top edge, mark with a

pencil where the back curve of the ear will sweep round to where it touches the bedding.

Slope the back of the ear down to the body, removing the waste with short strokes of the 8/7 for ease. At the base of the hind leg a bump has been left which we will use later to indicate the hind foot. The straw has been roughly stepped to shape. The back of the hind leg has been rounded back a little to give depth, and make it seem fuller. Sand with 180 grit.

5.22

5.22 To give a rough, crosshatched appearance to the straw, use the V-tool. All the cuts are done in random short blocks on the uneven surface that we left for this job. Broken ends, uneven bits and pieces, odd levels, and lines going every which way will make the straw look real. This is the one place where all those 'accidents' should happen on purpose.

Mark the continuation of the back of the ear and cut the undercut with the fishtail or the carving knife. Where the crate grooves meet up with the ear, use the 3/5 and the 5/3 to continue the grooves under the edge of the ear, then sand.

The right side of the crate can now be patterned to match the front as far as the tab: cut in the boards and undercut the straw. The undercutting of the rabbit and the straw is no different from the work already done on the flowers and leaves; the principle is the same regardless of the design.

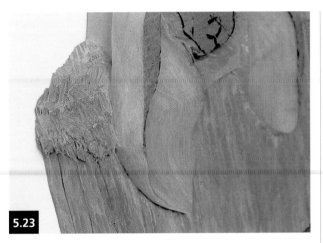

5.23

5.25

5.23 The left side is shaped by continuing the body down to meet the straw. The back of the ear is pencilled in first and then shaped with the fishtail, leaving the straw rough.

Pattern the straw and the side of the crate as far as the tab, undercutting the straw, as for the right side. Undercut the back of the ear, keeping the sweep full and soft. Continue the grooves on the crate to match. Leave the straw below the rabbit's face until later.

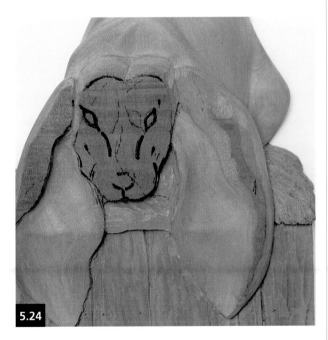

5.24

5.24 Sand over the entire back part of the rabbit, working back from the top of the head, progressing through the grades of paper for a fine finish. Do not sand the straw or the box.

5.25 The flat area of the right ear that so far has not been carved is now shaped back to the skull at the top; check the model for the finished depth. The front edge of the ear is then shaped; carve dips in it to create interest and contour, as well as rolling the edge in places. Sand it over to see how it looks, but do not undercut the flaps as they may get leant on and broken.

Carve the left ear in the same manner as the right, and sand over for clarity. Look closely at the left side of the face in the photograph: you can see that the waste from that side has been cut away, using the 3/5. The edge of the ear can now be seen, making the face more even.

On the right side of the cheek the 8/7 has been used to angle the face on a slope – check your model for the correct shape. Do not fuss over the section where the ear joins to the head – the detail of the ears will be the last thing to finish.

With the 9/10, cut a depression from between the eyes to the V at the top of the skull.

5.26

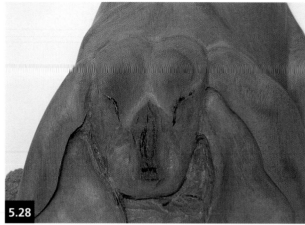

5.28

5.26 Carve the left side of the face in the same manner as the right side. Using the 8/7, cut a groove from below each eye to join into the line in the brow; it will look a bit like an upside-down Y.

Draw a pencil line through the pad of the nose as a centre line; from this, cut under the nose pad and round the lower cheeks and mouth area. Blend the shaping into the side of the face which you have already cut.

5.28 Sand the left side of the face to match the right, and sand the top of the skull above the eyes and the hard edge of the flat area. If there is a corner at the front edge of the skull, carve it away gently with the fishtail, then sand.

At the apex of the head – in the V at the back of the skull – use the 3/5 to cut a depression to give more shadow, then sand. Clearly mark in pencil the top line of the eyes, and with the fishtail cut an angle to remove the jutting ledge where the bottom of the eye will be. What we have done is to flatten the area that the eye sits in, sloping it down to meet the face.

From the blue oval, use the 9/10 to round the sharp ridge, as shown on the right side of the face. There is now a groove running down the right side to the nose pad.

Use the 9/10 on the left side of the blue oval, and cut it to match the right side so that the face is even. Trim the hard ridge under the left eye as for the right, using the fishtail as before.

Look at the nose pad: at the moment there is an angle that juts out just below the line of the drawing. With the fishtail, slice off the angle so that the pad is slightly rounded (convex), from below the pencil mark.

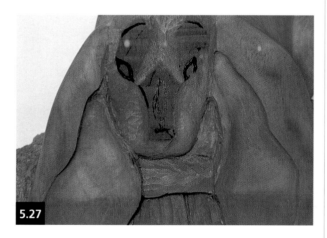

5.27

5.27 Work the left side of the face to match the right; take special care when carving near the edge of the left ear. Use the fishtail to soften or round over the edge of the Y, blending the hard edge away.

The right side of the face has been sanded for a better view and an oval has been drawn in blue pencil on the bridge of the nose: this marks the highest part of the face.

5.29

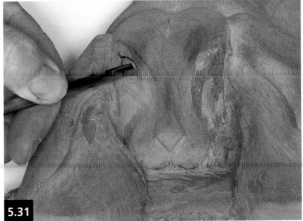

5.31

5.29 Sand over the entire face to get a clearer view of the timber and the shape.

Draw in the nose pad and the line underneath to the mouth line. From the corners of the nose draw an arc along the bridge, across the brow to where the ears join the face. This ensures that we can get the face even and the eyes level – any unevenness will be seen and can be adjusted now.

Pencil in the eyes clearly, making sure that they are level and the same size.

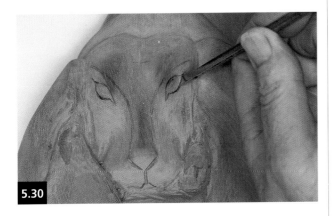

5.30

5.30 Use the V-tool to cut a V along both lines of the nose pad and down the division of the upper lip and mouth. This is no different from cutting a vein in a leaf.

When cutting in the eyes, use a chisel that matches the curve of the eye; it is not only the size of the chisel that matters, but the shape of the curve. In the photograph you can see that the 3/5 fits the curve and that it is being held at an angle to the timber while it is pushed in by hand.

5.31 When cutting the bottom eyelid the handle is held raised; when cutting the top eyelid the handle is lowered. This is so that the cuts are angled to give more depth, and the eyeball will sit behind the lids, not just poke out from them.

Work slowly; steady the hand holding the chisel against the timber for stability, and try to keep the pressure of the cuts at an even depth as you move along. Cut the full length of one lid before moving to the other. Use the 5/3 at the very tips of the corners, if needed, to remove any small specks that are hard to reach. To show you what we are aiming for, the right eye has been fully shaped with the chisels but not sanded.

Shave away any ridge left from the V-tool under the nose pad and sand the area. If the mouth has not yet been cut in, draw it in before cutting to make sure it ends up the shape you want.

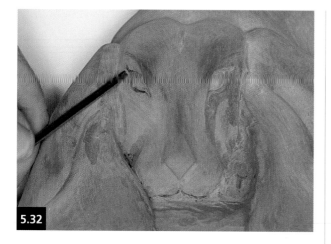

5.32

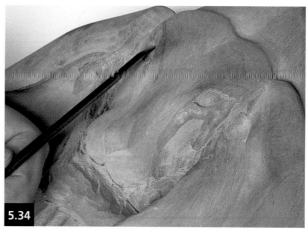

5.34

5.32 The left eye has had the cuts made along the pencil lines, as for the right eye. Now the 3/5 is being used to make the first cuts up under the lid. The hand is held slightly down – not straight on – so that the blade cuts up at an angle to the carving; this is done all along the line.

5.34 Follow the curve of the eyeball, using the 3/5 upside down, to shape the arc of the eye. Work slowly and gently, pushing only with the hand – do not use the mallet here, as the chisel may go too far. Work over the entire surface of the eye in this way.

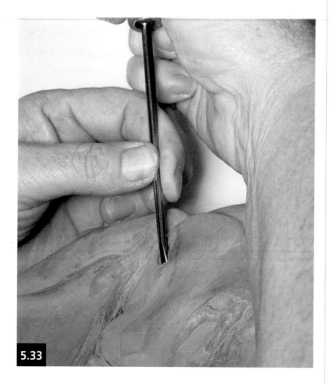

5.33

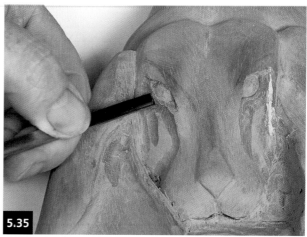

5.35

5.33 When forming the bottom undercut, the handle of the chisel is lifted. If it is easier for you, turn the carving upside down to cut the bottom line.

5.35 Cut a groove from the back of the eye with the 8/7, down the cheek to match the chalk mark visible on the right side of the face, and cut the groove that runs under the eye and down the face.

Taking the 3/5, carefully trim along the lower ridge of the eyelid to remove the sharp edge and match the right eye.

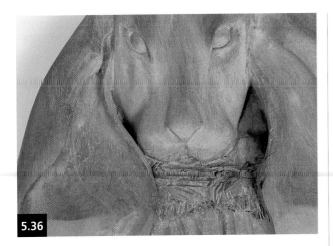

5.36

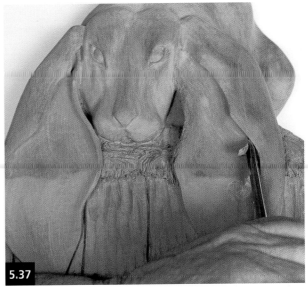

5.37

5.36 Cut the shape of the lip and mouth, using the 3/5 at an angle as we did when undercutting the eyelid. Remove a small amount from under the lip so the mouth sets back a little, and cut the curve of the chin. Sand the face all over.

Remove excess from along the side of the face, deepening the gap at the left to form a shadow. The right side is also cut back, and can either be carved to show a foot and leg as shown, or simply patterned as straw. The right ear is slightly undercut to give depth to this area. The recess is firstly stab cut with the 3/5, and then the waste removed with either the 3/5 or the 8/7. The leg, if carved, is left chisel-finished.

The straw at the front is cut in around the mouth and 'rough-cut' as before. The part that overhangs the crate can now be undercut and shaped.

5.37 The undercut of the roll or curve of the right ear is here being deepened; the entire ear can then be cleaned, finished and sanded. The left ear has already been trimmed, undercut and sanded. Sand the rabbit all over to a fine finish and remove the tabs.

Two ways to remove the tabs

1 If you have access to a bandsaw and are proficient in its use, you may saw one tab off just outside the line of the carving (making the cut in the waste). Holding the carving by the remaining tab, the corner of the crate can then be tooled and punched to match its surroundings. Saw the last tab in the same manner, then place a thick piece of leather under a clamp to secure and protect the crate while the last end is carved.

2 If a bandsaw is unavailable or you are concerned about damage, then use this method. Clamp at the left tab and use the fishtail to carefully lower the level of the right tab to the face of the carving. Cut a trench with the V-tool or a gouge and lower the level once again to the bottom of the cut. Keep working in this manner until half the thickness of the tab has been removed, leaving the level flat enough for the clamp to hold. Swap the clamp to the right tab and repeat the procedure on the left tab, this time working to a quarter of the original depth. Move the clamp back to the left tab; this time remove the last of the right tab and tool the end of the crate. Place a piece of heavy leather under the clamp to hold the crate while removing the last of the left tab and tooling the surface to match.

Colouring the eyes

It is a matter of preference whether you paint the eyes or leave them plain; I opted to paint them on this rabbit. I first rubbed one coat of oil over the entire carving to seal the surface. This will stop any bleeding of paint or absorption of moisture where it is not wanted.

Study the line drawing of the rabbit and take notice of the eyes and the shape of the iris. If the iris is drawn too small, the bunny will end up with little 'piggy' eyes and will look very mean. Try colouring copies of the drawing first, to see what looks good on your rabbit before you start on the carving itself.

I am using an artists' acrylic paint that comes ready to use in tube form; I find that woodstains in such small areas tend to bleed too much and there is not enough control.

5.38

5.38 For the large iris I have used burnt umber (dark brown), with Mars black for the centres. A small sable or other soft brush works well. Make sure that each coat is thoroughly dry before painting the next colour on. The difference in colour is hard to see before the oil is applied over the paint, but shows up quite well when it is finished.

Ensure that the paint has been allowed to harden before continuing with the oiling.

Oiling

I applied oil all over the project with a soft brush and then used a tightly rolled cloth to remove it from the crate and the straw. I applied two coats in this way, rubbing off both coats from the surface of the crate while still wet. For alternative methods, see Chapter 8.

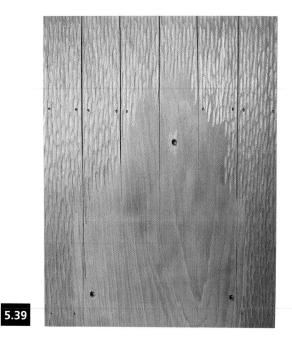
5.39

Carving the background

5.39 The backing is planed, cut to size, sanded, and the 1/4in (6mm) dowel holes drilled to a depth of 3/8in (9mm), using the template made earlier.

The backing board is carved in the same way as the crate. The rabbit is laid on the backing and a light pencil line drawn around him; with the rabbit removed, the lines are drawn for the boards and the tooling started. Each cut must pass beyond the outline of the rabbit, but there is no need to work the entire surface behind him. Finish with three coats of oil, brushed on and rubbed off as before.

Fix two triangular flap hangers 3in (75mm) down from the top edge and 1in (25mm) in from the sides. Attach picture wire so that it comes 1in (25mm) below the edge of the backing.

After checking the carving for fit, apply suitable glue to dowels and faces, position with care, place a weight on the project, and leave for 24 hours.

6 Koala

Camphor laurel has been used here for both the carving and the backing board. The backing has been cut from a sectional slice longways down the trunk, with the natural edge left on.

This timber is very popular for turners, carvers and furniture makers, as it tends to be very stable, polishes well, colours easily and carves crisply. It is a medium-density wood with a strong camphor aroma that I find refreshing – although some turners tend to find the smell overpowering.

The clay model

Once again we are going to complete the model and then take measurements from it to work from. Remember to wrap the clay in a plastic bag if leaving it for any length of time.

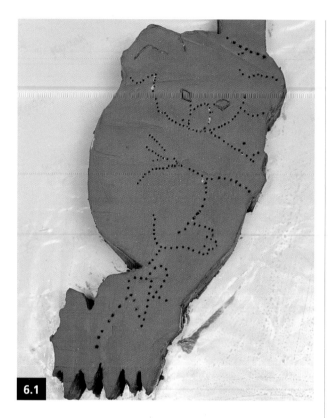

6.1

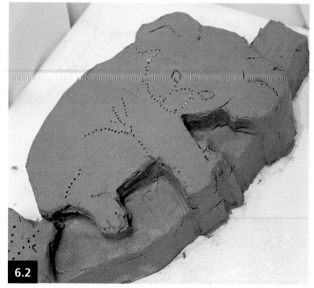

6.2

6.2 Use the skewer to draw a line ³⁄₄in (18mm) down from the top surface of the branch, then remove the clay to this level. Leave the leaves – we will attend to them later.

6.1 Make the basic model in the same way as we did for the bunny. It is essential that the model is the same thickness as the timber, or the measurements will not correspond.

When the clay block has been shaped and the paper design is still on top of it, use a skewer to prick holes along the inner design lines in exactly the same manner as we did for the rabbit, again to make it easy to draw the design onto the clay.

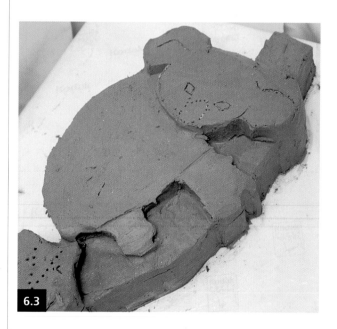

6.3

6.3 Cut down around the head and lower the entire body by ¹⁄₄in (6mm). Mark the beginning of the legs with a line as shown, and slope the clay down to the feet – they should be ¹⁄₈in (3mm) above the branch.

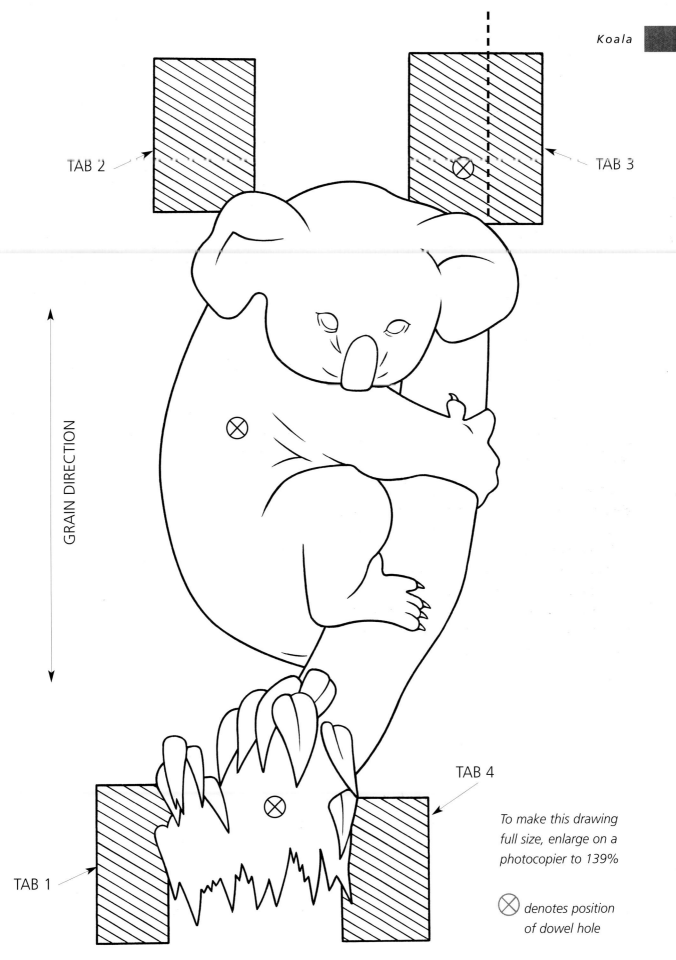

TAB 2

TAB 3

GRAIN DIRECTION

TAB 4

TAB 1

To make this drawing
full size, enlarge on a
photocopier to 139%

⊗ denotes position
of dowel hole

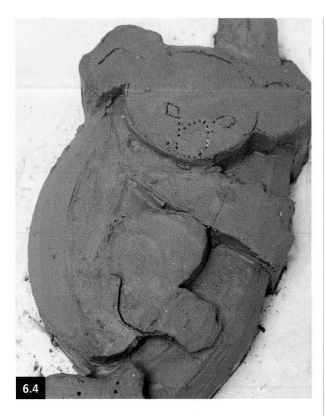

6.4

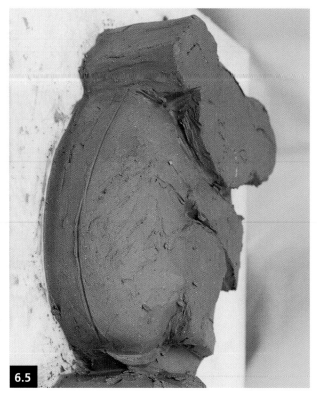

6.5

6.4 Remove a ¹/₂in (12mm) triangle of clay from between the ears at the top of the head. Cut a ¹/₄in (6mm) triangle from the outer edge of the branch. Cut a 1in (25mm) wedge from the koala's back to within 1¹/₂in (38mm) of the rump, sloping this to meet the corner at the base. Draw in the bend of the hind leg and take out a wedge of clay between front and hind legs. Remove clay from the top of the branch above the koala's head to match the rest of the tree.

6.5 Mark a line from the tip of the nose to the koala's back and cut clay down towards the ear from this mark, creating a hollow beneath the ear. At the deepest point at the bottom edge of the ear, the depth will be ¹/₂in (12mm), measured from the flat face of the clay at the edge of the ear.

Round the bottom by removing clay from behind the rear leg and rounding the haunch to meet up with the shaping of the back. The tip of the bottom is slightly below the left edge of the branch.

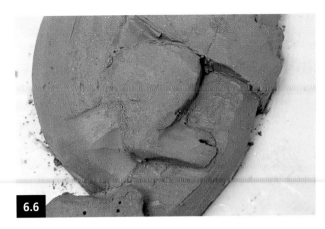

6.6

Round the thick part of the hind leg by removing the corner and the top and front edge. Lower the hock (ankle joint) by ¼in (6mm) and shape the foot to meet this level by scraping clay from the foot. This is done by removing the clay from the lower part of the foot which is nearest the branch.

6.6 To define the hind leg, cut clay away from the foot area and leave the toe area sloping down to meet the branch. Scrape clay from the inside edge of the branch to give contour, and smooth over with a spoon or knife.

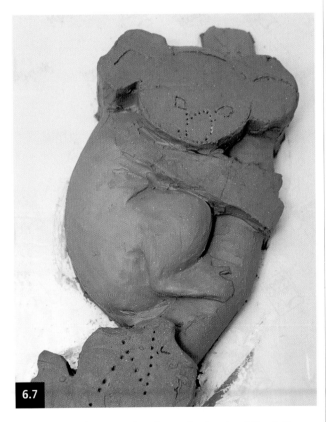

6.7

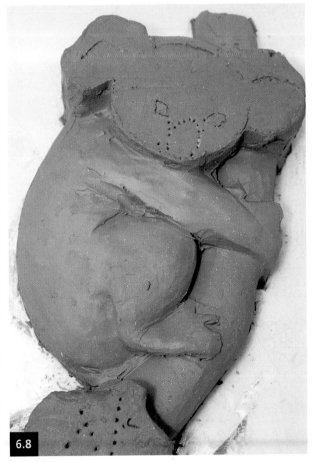

6.8

6.7 Mark a line starting from the back of the left ear at 1⅛in (29mm) above the baseboard to a mark at the buttocks at ¾in (19mm). Round the back and body to this line, keeping the fullness – do not scrape it flat but leave a soft, full curve. The rump should be lower than the shoulder.

6.8 Now shape the shoulder and front leg from nose to foot. First, remove clay from the outer edges of the arm to give a more rounded look. Remove the corners from the clay at the front foot and start to shape the contour to make it conform to the branch, as though it is holding on.

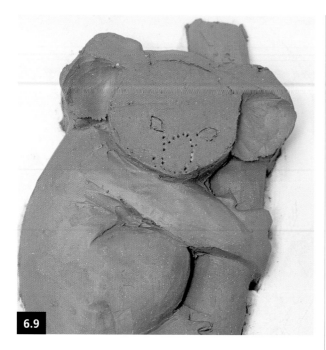

6.9

6.9 Shape the curve of the ears by using a teaspoon to scoop out the inner 'full' part, while leaving the heavy tops in place.

6.11

6.11 Remove a small amount of clay just above the nose, to lower the area between the eyes. Gently remove the corners from the tip and edges of the nose and round it slightly, keeping a 'flat' or 'blunt' look to it. Push in the flat end of the skewer to make the nostrils.

Mark where the eyes are located by pushing the flat end of the skewer into the clay. Roll small balls of clay and push these into the hollows to keep the location of the eyes.

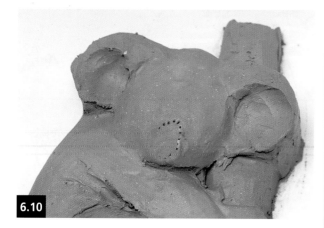

6.10

6.10 Round the tops of the ears by removing the square topmost edges. Do the same for the sides of the face, and round the top of the head to suit.

6.12

6.12 Turning to the left side at the back, undercut from the bottom to the top of the head. Round the back of the ears to form a cup shape, and remove excess clay from behind the ears for a smooth curve to the back.

6.13

6.13 Undercut the right side of the branch and the right ear. Shape the back of this ear to match the left one, to where it touches the top of the branch.

Continue the undercutting down to the leaves; undercut the rear leg slightly where it is full. Rough out the front foot and define the toes more on the hind leg.

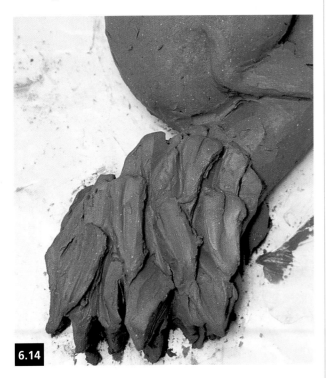

6.14

6.14 Lower the leaf block to 1¹/₂in (38mm), and cut out chunks at random so that a multi-level look remains. It does not have to be perfect – this is simply a guide at this stage, and the leaves will be clarified later.

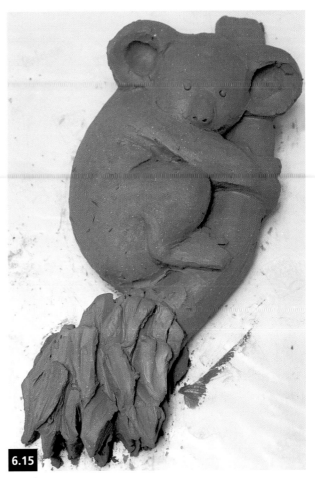

6.15

6.15 The clay model is now complete. From now on all measurements will be taken directly from the clay model and transferred to the relevant position on the timber with the use of a skewer and a ruler, in the same manner as we did for the rabbit.

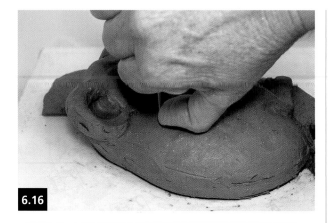

6.16

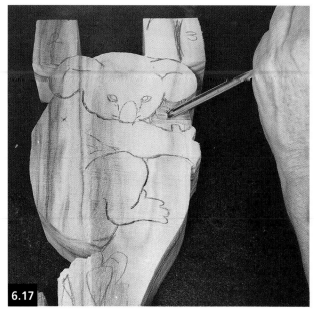

6.17

6.16 To measure the thickness of the model, use a skewer to pierce the clay all the way through to the backing board – keeping the skewer upright – and then place your thumbnail against the spot where it emerges from the clay. Withdraw the skewer slowly without moving your thumbnail, and measure the distance from end of skewer to thumbnail. This is what the thickness of the timber needs to be at this position. By measuring the position on the model and then transferring that measurement to the timber we have a way to 'depth-gauge' how far the timber needs cutting back. For full control, repeated depth-testing is done in each section that is carved, just as we did for the rabbit.

No undercutting will be attempted until the whole project is completed.

Carving the timber

It is assumed that the clay model will be depth-tested at each stage before cutting the timber.

Note that at times the clamps have been removed to allow clearer access for photography.

Trace the design onto the timber and bandsaw the profile, retaining the tabs intact.

Turn the project face down; hold with a clamp and drill three 1/4in (6mm) holes for the dowels that are marked on the line drawing.

Stab-cut the outline of the koala's head, including where it touches the tabs and the branch. Use either the fishtail or the 3/5, turning it to conform to the shape as you cut. Cut the lines of both legs and feet in the same manner.

6.17 Test the depth of the clay with your skewer at the centre of the branch between the right ear and front foot; note the measurement and mark this depth onto the outer side of the timber. Move along the branch to the centre of the next section and repeat, measuring and marking until the leaves are reached. Join the pencil marks on the outer edge of the timber until you have a continuous line from the leaves to the ear.

Use the 8/7 chisel to reduce the timber all along the branch until it reaches this new level, taking care not to remove the feet or toes.

6.18

6.18 The level of the branch has now been reduced to the pencil mark, leaving the feet and ears untouched. There is no need at this stage to fuss over small chips or other debris; that will come later.

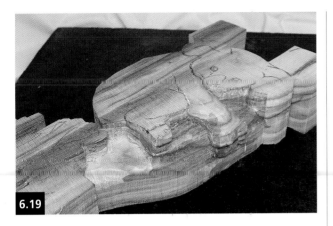

6.19

6.19 Cut off the sharp corner of the branch with either 9/10, 8/7 or fishtail. Use the fishtail to round the edge all the way from ear to leaves.

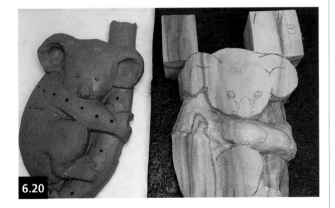

6.20

6.20 From the nose to the front foot of the model, repeatedly test for thickness along the arm; these measurements are used to determine how much timber is cut away. Pare timber away with the fishtail until the arm is the same shape as the model, testing repeatedly with ruler and skewer. Watch that the shoulder bone is left high. Slope the wood down to the ear as on the model.

Use a pencil to mark the position of the front foot where the koala is holding the branch, and remove the unwanted wood from below it. If unsure how big to leave the foot, allow extra – it will be easier to see the correct size when more detail has been carved.

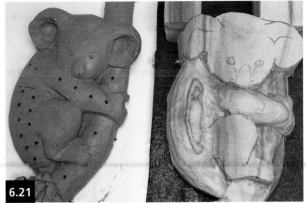

6.21

6.21 Use the 8/7 gouge to remove the bulk of the hollow that forms a V between the front and hind legs. Use the V-tool to clarify the sharp edges and the deeper point.

Mark a pencil line from the top of the hind leg across the body to the back, 1¾in (44mm) down below the ear. Check the depth every ½in (12mm) along the centre of this section from the back to the hand. Use either the fishtail or the 8/7 to cut the timber to match.

Continue to work down along the back to the rump, testing the clay for depth before cutting the timber to match. Start from the left or outer edge first, and work down and then further into the carving. Use the 9/10 or 8/7, then smooth off with the fishtail.

There will be times when the section that you are working on will look 'odd'. It is important that you trust in the measurements from the clay model – if they are followed all the way through, then the carving will work out.

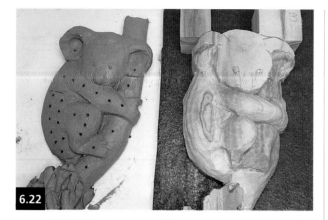

6.22

6.24

6.22 Test the thickness of the hind leg and foot. Use the 8/7 to reduce waste, then smooth off with the fishtail. Use the fishtail to round the plump part of the leg, turning the tool upside down and cutting with the inside of the blade along the front curve.

Cut alongside the head at the ear with the 8/7, and use the same tool to scoop out the inner ear, leaving a rounded surface.

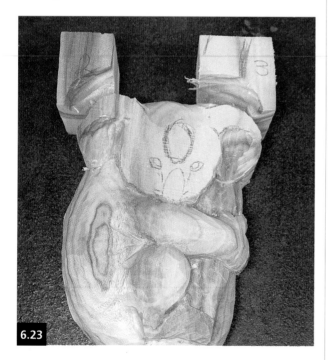

6.23

6.23 Cut a trench in tabs 2 and 3 just outside the lines of the design, using either gouge. Do not cut tab 3 below the level of the branch.

Cut a small trench with the V-tool or the 8/7 in the top of the head at the junction with the ears. Mark the high point of the head with a pencilled oval.

6.24 Pare the timber back from this mark to round the top of the head, leaving the oval as the highest point of the face, as on the model.

Gently stab-cut around the nose; do not cut very deep, or the marks will show later. Working from the oval pencil mark, cut towards the nose down at an angle, using the 3/5 to curve the wood slightly into the nose.

Use the 8/7 and start to round the edge of the face all the way around from ear to ear; work from whichever angle your timber cuts best. The finishing of the face will be left until last.

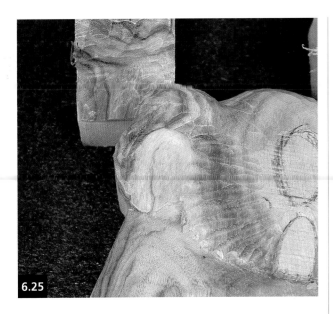

6.25

6.25 Widen the trench in tab 2 to give access to the top of the ear. Use either the inside or the outside of the fishtail to curve the top edge of the ear. Deepen the inside of the ear with the 9/10 if required.

Once satisfied with the final shape, go over lightly with the 8/7 to leave small ridges in the direction of the heavy hair. Undercut the front edge of the ear where it touches the neck with the 3/5. Tool marks in this area will be left, not sanded away.

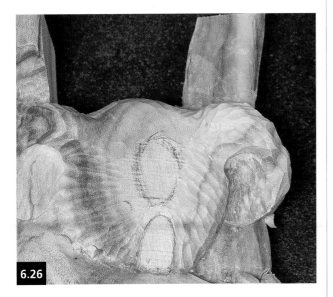

6.26

6.26 Mark the continuation of the branch in tab 3 above the right ear. Cut the timber down to branch level only, so that the branch continues above the head. Trim off the excess timber from the tab.

Round the top of the branch, then move to the outer edge of the branch and pencil in the outer curve of the right ear.

Remove the excess wood from the branch under the right ear, so that the branch seems to continue behind it. Undercut the full length of the branch from leaves to top, using the fishtail.

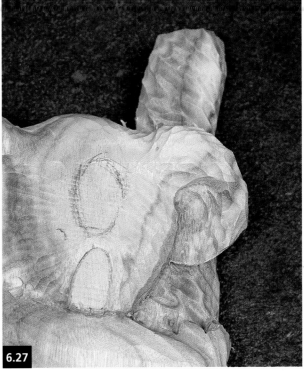

6.27

6.27 Pattern the branch by cutting with the 8/7 gouge at an angle along its full length, following the surface curvature to give a twisted look to the surface of the branch. Use short strokes, as we did on the rabbit's crate, to give the branch a rough, random appearance.

Undercut the right ear where it touches the branch with the 3/5 or 5/3, and similarly along the right side of the face to leave it tidy.

Tidy the front leg with the fishtail if required. Check the contours before undercutting a small amount all around. Mark the toes in pencil before cutting in with the 3/5, allowing for the claws (which are long, thin extensions of the toes). Koalas have five toes: two close together, then a space and three more, almost like an elongated hand. Undercut all the toes slightly, enough to show their contour. Continue to pattern the branch to match the surrounding area, undercutting with the 3/5 and 5/3 as needed.

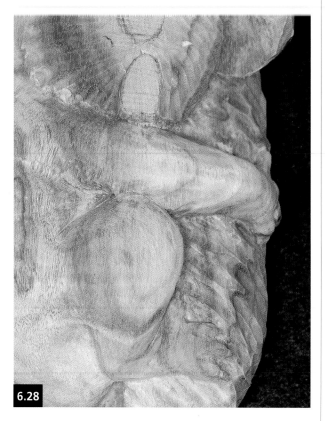

6.28

6.28 Cut in the hind foot with the fishtail, shape the toes as for the front foot and undercut to match. Work the branch to match the existing part, as far as the leaves.

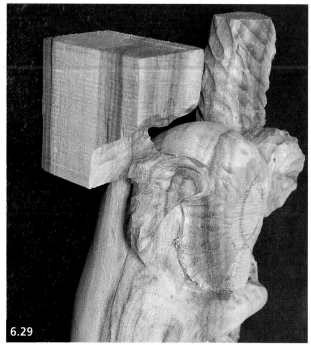

6.29

6.29 Deepen the trench in tab 2 with the 8/7 but do not remove it yet. Mark the outside of the left ear and cut away the waste from under the back of the ear; this involves cutting into the tab.

Use the fishtail to undercut all along the back and behind the head and neck. Use the 8/7 to undercut the tab, leaving a 'bridge' still connected to the ear.

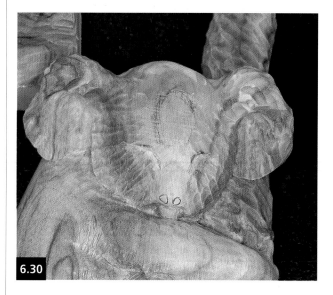

6.30

6.30 If you feel that the face needs extra depth, then deepen the ears with the 8/7 or 9/10. This allows the edges of the fur of the face to be lowered, giving more depth. If the face requires more rounding, cut the outer area lower with the 8/7. Stab-cut with the 3/5 to undercut slightly where face and front leg meet, and where the face meets the branch on the right side.

The nose is broad and slightly bulbous, with large, open, forward-facing nostrils. Gently, and using the 3/5, cut towards the face and pare the closest edge in to the face to give it a soft rounding or dome shape. Round the outer edges and remove the square corner at the front edge.

Mark with a pencil a quarter of the way up from the bottom of the nose area and stab-cut to form the division between nose and mouth. Draw in the chin before cutting in with the 3/5. Lower the chin a little so that it sits below the level of the nose, and carve it into a rounded shape to form a small cup.

Sand the nose and pencil in the nostrils and the ridge above the eyes.

Use the 8/7 to cut a small groove following under the ridge of the eyes, below the pencil mark. With the fishtail, cut off the tops off the heavier grooves of the face.

Brush over the body and ears (but not the nose) with the brass-wire brush to simulate the very dense hair of the koala. The nose pad is smooth and hairless, so leave this as it is.

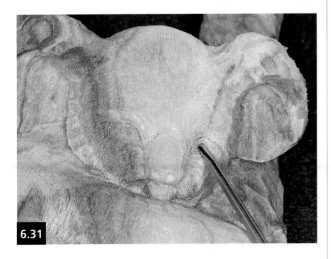

6.31

6.31 Pencil the eyes in and use the 3/5 to cut them in; do not cut very deep. Lower the handle of the tool as you round off the eyeballs.

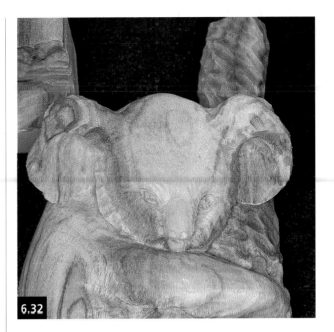

6.32

6.32 The nostrils are drilled in with the 1/8in (3mm) drill, held almost at the same angle as the chisel in photograph 6.31. Clean away the lower front edges with the 5/3, and sandpaper.

Cut away the rest of tab 2 and clean the area to match the work already completed.

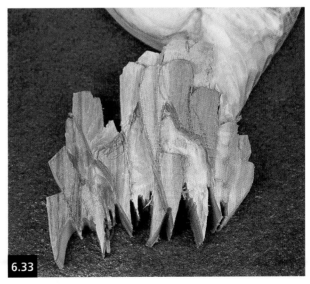

6.33

6.33 Pencil in some definition on the group of leaves, and stab-cut around the leaves that are to remain on the highest level. Using the 3/5, lower the area between the top leaves by 1/4in (6mm).

While the face of the leaves is still flat, hold it with the clamp and cut away the last two tabs.

6.34

6.36

6.34 Using the 8/7 cut a trench in the leaves so that some continuation of the branch can be carved. Do not cut all the way through the leaf group – this allows some leaves to remain at the rear for extra depth. The rear set of leaves can now be randomly profiled by cutting angles and shapes into them with the V-tool; then sand lightly.

6.36 Use the V-tool, the fishtail or the 3/5 to profile the face of the leaves. Don't forget to vary the angle of some of the leaves by cutting one side lower than the other. Sand lightly to remove any fuzz or other loose debris.

6.35

6.35 Mark another level of leaves on the front group and lower these also, using the 3/5 and/or the V-tool. This will create a ragged group, typical of gums, when the faces of the leaves are shaped.

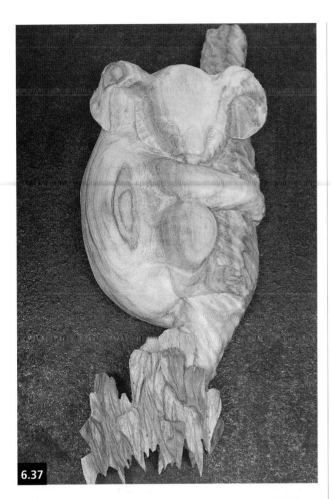

6.37

6.38

6.39

6.37 and 6.38 Although the koala is completed, to me he looks a little 'blind'. You must decide whether you wish to colour his nose and eyes. I have applied one coat of Danish oil to seal the surface of the timber, allowed it to dry and then painted both eyes and nose with artists' black acrylic, using a small sable brush.

The carving is now ready to be oiled. I chose to brush on two coats of Danish oil and allow it to dry.

The backing

6.39 I have chosen a slab of camphor laurel for the backing; any timber larger than the carving would do the job. The timber has been planed and had the outer edges darkened by rubbing a stain mix over it.

After the template was situated and the holes drilled for the dowels as usual, a strip of tape was laid over the area that the carving will cover; this is to keep the oil from adhering, to allow better grip for the glue.

After the backing has been oiled and allowed to dry, attach two flap hangers before dowelling the carving to the backing. Leave to set for 24 hours with a suitable weight to hold it in place.

7 Tree frog

TIMBER

Carving: Borneo teak, 6½ x 11¾in
(165 x 300mm) x 2in (50mm) thick

Backing: lime, oval, 9½ x 12½in
(241 x 318mm) x ⅝in (16mm) thick

Borneo teak was my choice for the frog because of the definite lines or stripes in the timber. Don't be deterred by the natural colours that are in various timbers, as often they can work in your favour. This timber is fairly soft and cuts easily, but does tend to be a little 'hairy'. This results in the need for sanding – this timber is not recommended for a chisel finish.

Any timber of contrasting colour could be used for the backing, but lime would have to be one of the most preferred timbers for woodcarvers worldwide. It cuts cleanly and crisply without a great deal of effort, holds detail extremely well and can be sanded or left with a chisel finish. It does on occasion have small faults in it, but these are overlooked as being indigenous to the craft. It is well worth using this timber on any carving project.

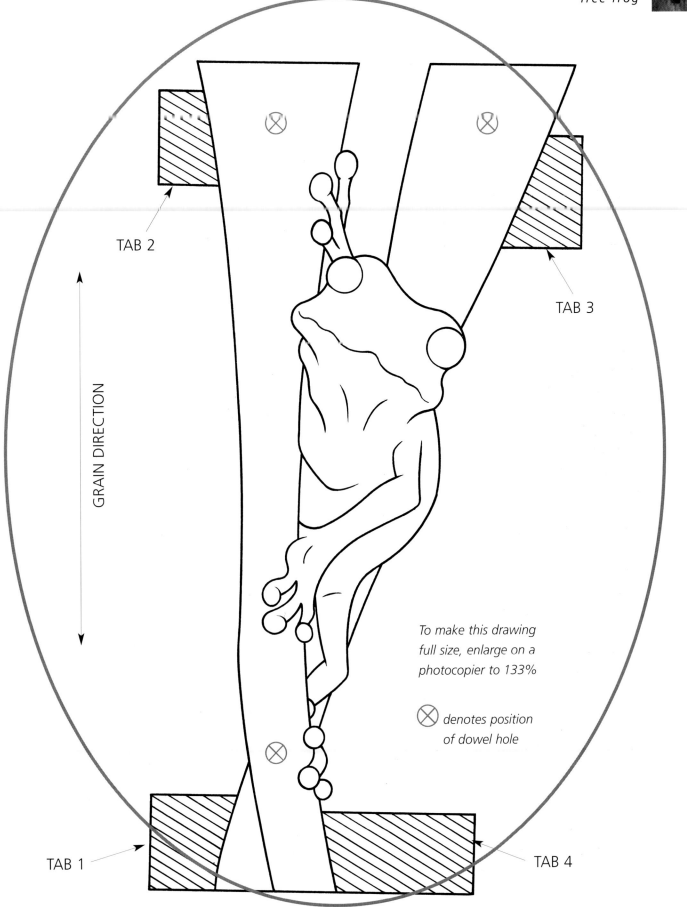

TAB 2

GRAIN DIRECTION

TAB 3

To make this drawing
full size, enlarge on a
photocopier to 133%

⊗ denotes position
of dowel hole

TAB 1

TAB 4

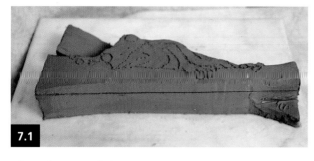

7.1

The clay model

7.1 Make a basic model in the usual way, pricking the design through the paper to leave the details prominent. The frog is clinging to a type of cane and is actually between the two stalks, the piece on the right being the furthest away.

Scribe a line along the right-hand side of the clay, 1in (25mm) up from the baseboard (that is, half the thickness of the clay) at the top end, sloping down to 3/4in (19mm) at the lower end. Reduce the clay on the right-hand stalk to this mark. Do not remove clay from behind the frog.

Mark the left stalk on the outside 1⁵/₈in (41mm) thick at the top, sloping down to 1¹/₄in (32mm) at the bottom.

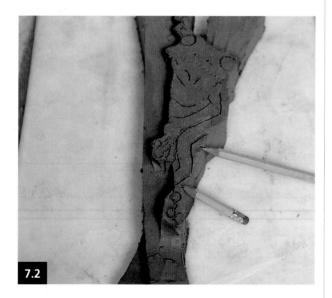

7.2

7.2 Lower the clay on the left stalk, working slowly so as not to remove the detail of the toes. Note the small sections on the right where the pencils are pointing: these areas are part of the right stalk and need to be reduced to the line made earlier.

7.3

7.3 Round the edges of the stalks by removing a little clay from the corners. On the top (wider) section of the right-hand stalk the leaf has been 'stepped' to give more contour and to add interest. This is done by dragging a V-shaped piece of wood through the clay repeatedly. Do not undercut.

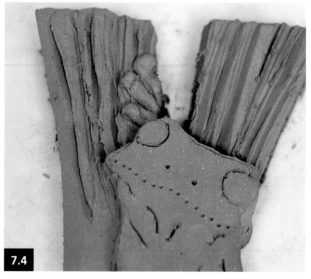

7.4

7.4 Treat the top of the left leaf in the same manner, only sloping it down towards the centre – making sure you leave enough clay for the foot. Sloping the clay down on the inside makes it easier to get the foot situated.

For the upper foot (above the head), lower the clay to 1/8in (3mm) above the leaf and shape the fingers. The frog's 'hands' have definite fingers, with round and bulbous tips; they should look as though they are holding onto the stalk.

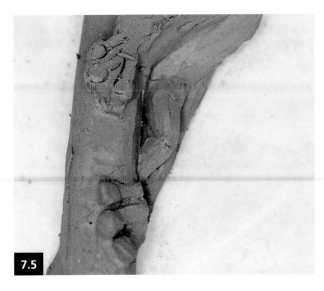

7.5

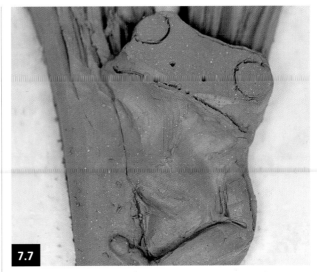

7.7

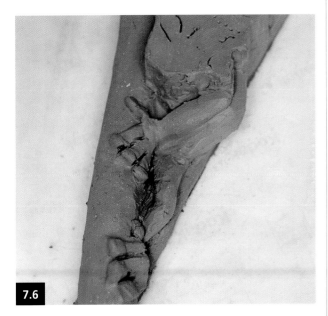

7.6

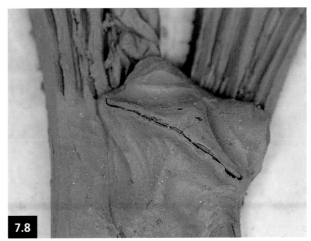

7.8

7.5 Do the same for the bottom foot, remembering that these do not have to be perfect as the model is only a guide. Set in the hind leg and the belly so it all fits in place, working only as far as the shoulder.

7.6 Notice that part of the frog's chest protrudes in front of the stalk. The lower chest area is below the level of the stalk and creates a hollow where it joins on to the abdomen. Shape the lower hand and arm up to the elbow.

7.7 The centre of the mouth is the highest point (the furthest forward); from here the mouth curves back to the corners. Reduce the clay at each corner of the mouth until the correct curve has been achieved, then redraw the mouth line. Now that the mouth profile has been established, the chin and throat area can be set in. Keep in mind that frogs have a 'baggy' throat and that on these fellows wrinkles look good.

Scrape the clay in the direction that you wish to form the wrinkles, leaving a ridge below the mouth for the jawbone. Fit the top of the arm to suit.

7.8 The nostrils are sited on the high ridge of the face, which slopes down on both sides to the outer jaw and back to the top of the head. Scrape the clay away to obtain the shape, then roughly round the eyes.

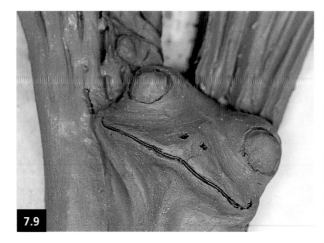

7.9

7.9 Mark in the eyes using a skewer or kebab stick, leaving them very bulbous so that they protrude. The model is now complete and ready for us to measure from.

The carving

Drill three ³/₄in (6mm) holes for the dowels in the back of the timber and make the template; this is easy to do while the wood is flat.

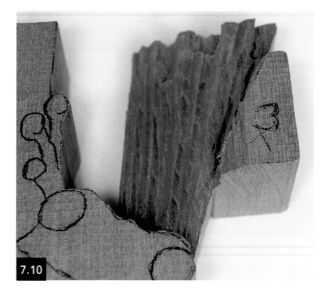

7.10

7.10 With either a chisel or the knife, stab-cut along the line of the design above the frog's head, and between the leaf and tab 3. Lower the top of the leaf to match the clay.

Notice that the ends of the leaf have been profiled by using the V-tool repeatedly to give an irregular depth and look to the leaf.

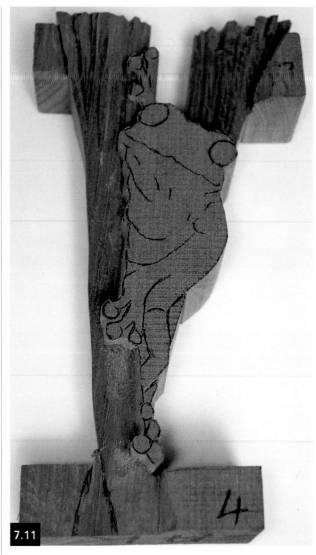

7.11

7.11 Stab-cut the left side of the design, taking care when working around the toes. Lower the level on this side and round the stalk with the fishtail. Match the top of the leaf by again cutting with the V-tool.

7.12

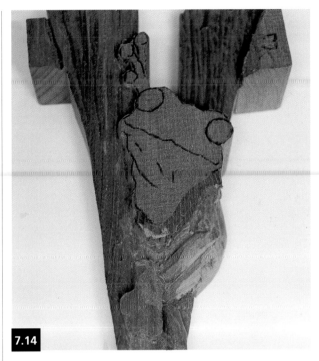

7.14

7.12 Stab-cut along the lower edge of the arm and reduce the level of the timber with the 3/5 until the belly has been reached; then redraw the details.

7.14 Stab-cut along the line of the arm and reduce the arm to the required level (checked from the model). Use the 8/7 to reduce the bulk of the waste from under the chest until the level of the arm is reached; revert to the 5/3 and the 3/5 to cut the area between arm and belly.

Cut away the sharp outer edge of the belly with the fishtail to round it off.

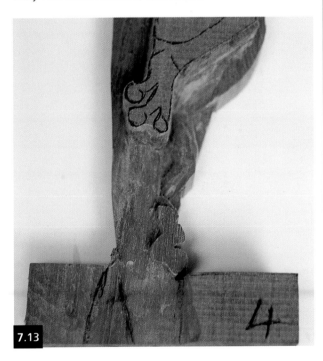

7.13

7.13 Cut in the leg and the lower levels of the stalk with either the 3/5 or the 5/3; the groin will be the lowest area shown. The details of the hands and feet will be left until last.

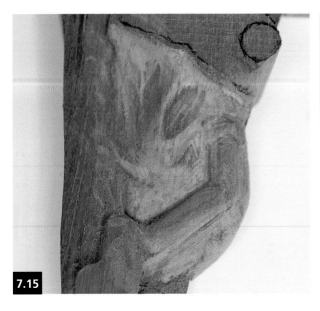

7.15

7.15 Use the 9/10 to shape the contour of the jawbone, leaving enough of a ridge underneath for the chin and lip. Cut the sagging skin under the throat and upper chest with either the 9/10 or the 8/7 and blend it into the belly area. Sand lightly to clarify the details.

7.16

7.16 Using the 3/5, lower the height of the top hand above the stalk to ¹/₈in (3mm); then leave it for the moment.

When shaping the face of the frog, cut away only small amounts of wood at a time, and step back now and then to get the work into perspective.

Use the 8/7 to relieve the wood from between the eyes and round the top of the head, ensuring that plenty of timber is left for the eyes to protrude from the face.

The 8/7 is also used to cut the groove that runs from above the side of the mouth, below the eyes and up to the ridge of the nose; check with the clay model at regular intervals for measurements. Pencil in the eyes again but do not cut them yet.

7.17

7.17 Redraw the details of the fingers of the upper hand on the timber. If you feel that there is insufficient wood to fit the hand in, then lower the whole area of the upper frond. Canting this area towards the centre will allow a larger amount of timber for the fingers and hand. Redraw the details.

Tabs 2 and 3 can now be removed.

Slope the back of the head down towards the right frond – this needs cutting back only enough so that it cannot be seen from the front – then sand. Sand the whole face, round the eyes so that the bulbous shape is very definite, and make sure that they are of equal size.

7.18

7.18 Trim excess from around the fingers and the back of the hand with either the 3/5 or the 5/3. Take very small cuts and work slowly so the timber does not splinter away from the design.

Continue to remove the waste gently from around the fingers until the shape has been cleared; when stab-cutting around the fingers take care not to cut too deeply, so as not to mark the lower timber.

Use the 8/7 to cut the depression between the soft ends and the fingers; the photograph shows the ends of the fingers being shaped using the 3/5.

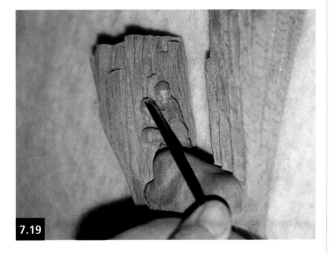

7.19

7.19 The inside curve of the 3/5 is here being used to round the top edges, cutting across the grain at an angle to lessen the chance of splintering. Sand the hand all over for clarity.

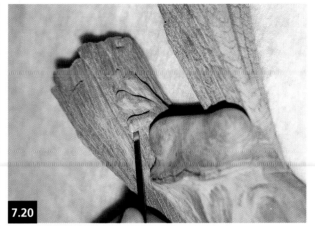

7.20

7.20 When you are satisfied with the fingers they can be undercut gently using the 5/3, the principles being the same as for the previous projects.

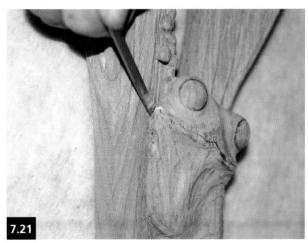

7.21

7.21 Pencil in the eyes, but do not cut them yet. I find that if they are drawn in and then left awhile, any lack in symmetry will be noticed when we return.

Undercut the side of the face, neck, and chest areas where they touch the stalk, and sand the area under the jaw.

7.22

7.22 Draw in the mouth if necessary and, using either the carving knife or the 5/3 or 3/5, cut in the mouth line. The photograph shows the left side of the mouth cut in an irregular line by stab-cutting with the 3/5 chisel, turning it to follow the contour as required. The edge is then pared away carefully with the same chisel so as to open the gap slightly. Sand gently.

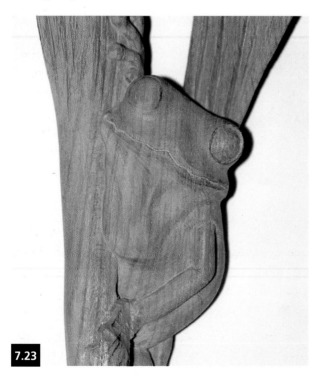

7.23

7.23 Cut the right side of the mouth to match the left, and sand the area gently. Continue to sand the stomach, stalk and arm down to the lower hand, and draw the details of the fingers ready for cutting.

Clean up if required any small rubbish between hind leg and stalk, then sand the lower belly and hind leg down to the back foot.

Cut the eyes in the same manner as for the bunny and the koala – the only difference here is that the eyes are round and bulbous. Ensure that the chisel used (5/3) fits the curve of the eye, or there will be unsightly marks left all around the eyeball. Use the same chisel or the 3/5 to round the ball of the eye. The photograph shows the right eye cut in but not yet sanded.

Cut the left eye to match the right before sanding both of them together; this makes it easier to get them to match up.

7.24

7.24 Cut the lower hand in the same manner as the top hand, by removing the waste and cutting the pads in first, before shaping the fingers and sanding. Do the same for the lower foot, cutting away only enough of tab 4 to allow access to the toes. Sand all over and, when satisfied, cut away tab 1.

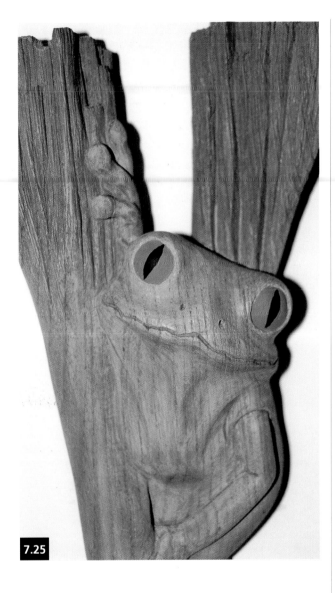

7.25

7.25 Mark the nostrils in with pencil, and then drill the two holes using a 1/32in (0.8mm) drill.

Wet to raise grain, sand and dry.

Painting the eyes is optional. I have oiled the carving with one coat of Danish oil to seal the timber before using artists' acrylic raw sienna to hide the stripes in the timber. Mars black was used for the slits, which can be either horizontal or vertical – both are correct. As our irises widen in the dark and shrink in the light, so do frogs' eyes, with the exception that theirs close to a slit, depending on the species.

The last remaining tab is now cut way and the area sanded. The entire carving was then finished with Danish oil. This was rubbed onto the stalks, but left thick on the frog to make him look shiny and wet.

The backing

Since drawing ovals can be difficult for those not familiar with the task, I suggest that you find a friendly picture framer near you. When they cut mounts (coloured cardboard surrounds) for photos and paintings, they throw away the centre part where the picture sits. If you ask, they will often sell or give you the centres of ovals and circles, and you can use these as templates to mark your backboards. It saves a lot of time.

Cut the oval and mark in pencil 1/4in (6mm) from the back and 1/2in (12mm) in from the front edge. Bevel the edge back to these two marks in the same manner as used previously.

The backing in this case was given one coat of Danish oil and allowed to dry thoroughly; then the bevel only was sanded back to bare timber. The bevel then had one application of Contemporary Maple stain applied to it and allowed to dry. Coating the timber with one layer of oil beforehand allowed the stain to be confined to the one area, without bleeding onto the face of the wood.

When dry, the backing can be re-oiled in the normal manner, the hanger attached and the frog glued on with the dowels.

8 Finishing your work

Staining

The use of stain on timber is not new, but the variety of stains now available gives a myriad of choices to the woodworker. Although stains come labelled with their own instructions, with a little imagination the possibilities are endless.

Precautions when using stains

- *Ensure that you read the labels on each container and identify what the solvent is for each one. Do not mix water-based stains with solvent-based ones; oil and water still do not mix.*
- *Do not smoke while using solvents or stains.*
- *Do wear rubber gloves to protect sensitive skin.*

REQUIREMENTS

- a variety of stains having the same solvent base
- a small quantity of the appropriate solvent
- an eye dropper
- brushes, preferably soft hair such as sable or squirrel.

FOLIAGE PROJECT (SEE CHAPTER 3)

If you prefer not to colour the leaves, proceed to oil them as described on page 97.

8.1

8.1 Because the leaves cut from jelutong are very pale and the rosewood backing very rich in colour, I felt the contrast was too sharp. By adding colour to the leaves it is possible to alter the whole look of the finished piece.

Take a few offcuts of the same timber that the leaves were cut from; these will be used to test the colour mixes.

Have available a number of small, clean containers (such as bottle lids), having first checked that they will not melt in the solvent that is listed on the stain containers.

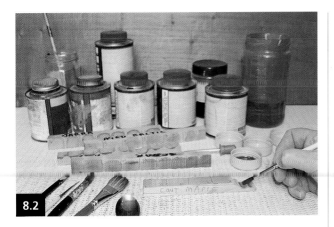

8.2 Place a spoonful of solvent into a lid.

Take two drops of stain from one tin using an eye dropper, add them to the solvent and mix together. Test this mix on the waste wood by dipping a soft brush in the mix and lightly touching it to the wood. Write on the wood the name of the stain (such as Cedar), and the number of drops of colour.

Keep adding stain and testing in this way. Try another stain, using a fresh lid, and continue to number the tests.

When the stain swatches are dry, the choices available are easy to see – just remember that the colour will vary slightly with oiling, usually becoming a little darker and more intense.

Photo 8.2 shows multiple test swatches made for the jelutong; the stains tested were called Cedar, Walnut, Jarrah, Contemporary Maple, Aged Baltic and Teak.

To clarify the final choice, it helps to oil these samples and save them. Next time this timber is used it will only remain to study the samples and make a choice. Every type of wood will colour differently, so you will need to make a separate set of samples for each of the paler timbers that you are likely to stain.

When applying more than one colour, allow the first to dry before adding more, or they will merge – unless, of course, that is the effect you want.

Once the colours have been tested on the timber, a decision can be made. It only remains to select the finished colour by name and the dilution ratio by number: for example, 'Cedar 4' would indicate Cedar stain with four drops to the teaspoonful.

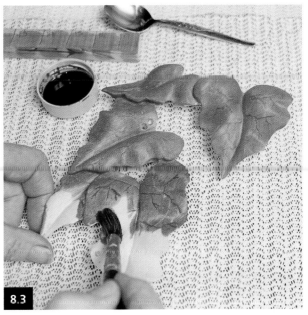

8.3 Load a soft brush with the first mix and, starting on the open areas of the leaves near the central vein, lay the colour on by lightly touching the fully loaded brush against the timber, rather than painting it on as you would if applying it to the wall of a house.

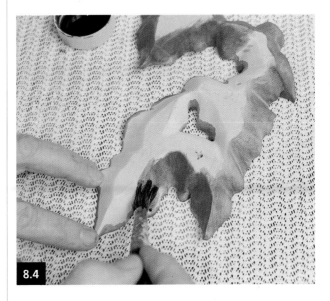

8.4 Stain all the undercut parts at the back in the same way.

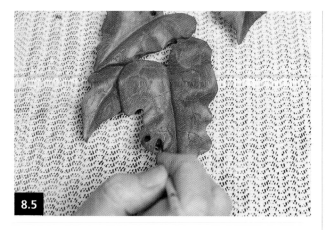

8.5

8.5 Make sure the timber is dry before using the second mix. With a finer brush colour the bug holes, tipping the work slightly so the stain bleeds into the wood where the concentration of colour is wanted.

8.6

8.7

8.6 and 8.7 Extra colour can be added to the veins and around the edges. Add a little black, if wanted, in the same manner. Add more or less colour to

make the carving individually suit the timber and your own tastes.

For the leaves in the Foliage project I used the following order of application:

1 Cedar stain, 12 drops per spoonful: main body and back of carving

2 Jarrah stain, 10 drops per spoonful: veins and bug holes

3 Jarrah stain, full strength: edges of leaves

4 Black stain, full strength: used sparingly on edges. When satisfied with the colours, allow to dry thoroughly before oiling.

FLOWER AND LEAF PANEL (SEE CHAPTER 4)

8.8

8.8 I stained the entire project with Cedar stain: two coats front and back, applied with a clean brush. Follow the instructions on the can; this time the stain is not diluted.

This leaves both the front and the backing dark. To give a little more 'life' and show the highlights of the carving, we can now soften the effect.

Fold some clean cotton cloth into a tight wad and dip it into solvent (stain reducer), then rub the dampened wad over the higher points of the carving, but not the backing. Repeat as often as required to get the desired effect. The lower areas will remain dark, but the higher profiles will stand out with the reduction of density.

When dry, oil using one of the methods described in the next section. I chose to paint on two coats of Danish oil with a clean brush, rub back lightly with 0000 steel wool when hard, and apply another coat of oil with a brush. A further coat of oil was then rubbed on to hide any possible brush strokes, and allowed to harden in a dust-free area.

Oiling

I know of no hard-and-fast rules on how a carving should be finished, or what to finish it with. With so much to choose from it is just a question of personal choice. One good-quality oil is sufficient for the moment; you can experiment with others later on.

Danish oil is simple to use, reasonably priced and gives a nice lustre to carvings when applied with the 'rubbed' method. If a hard, more glossy finish is required, Danish oil may still be used; in this case apply more liberally with a brush, and cut back with steel wool between coats.

PREPARATION

The more time and effort is spent on preparing the timber before it is oiled, the better the finished result.

Very soft timbers can tend to look 'woolly' after they have been oiled. If particular attention is not paid to the project at preparation time, it will look rough when it is finished.

There are no shortcuts; a minimum of three grades of sandpaper must be used to obtain a good finish. Some timbers may require working through five grades of paper; skimping on time and effort will show up when oil is applied.

8.9

8.9 When applying oil, use only clean, soft cloth that has been rolled into a tight bun. (The timber

shown here is the rosewood backing for the Foliage panel in Chapter 3.)

The cloth may be formed into a point to get into hard-to-reach areas, or a tight sausage shape for small grooves. Old, clean, soft T-shirt material or sheets are ideal, as they will not scratch or leave lint behind.

Do not flood the cloth or the timber with oil, but keep adding oil to the cloth as the timber absorbs it and it is rubbed in. Make sure that the oil is evenly applied; if 'ponds' appear, use a dry spot on the cloth to absorb excess oil. Leave at least 24 hours to harden in a dust-free area.

For soft wood that has had thinned stain applied, rub back carefully with steel wool, or just rub dry with cloth.

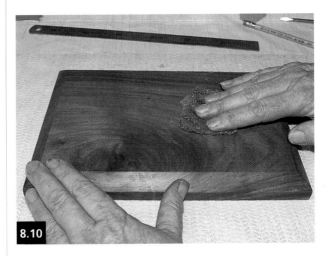

8.10

8.10 Check that the oiled timber is hard and dry before rubbing over with either 0000 or 000 steel wool. Do not add any oil or lubricant to the steel wool, but rub the entire oiled surface. Take care that the pressure is kept even when rubbing or it will finish up blotchy.

Use a clean paintbrush or the blower on the vacuum cleaner to help remove the dust fragments before applying another coat of oil.

Repeat until satisfied with results. Some timbers will require more work than others; trial and error is the only way to find out.

If stain of any type is to be applied, then it must be done before oiling; allow the timber to dry thoroughly before oiling.

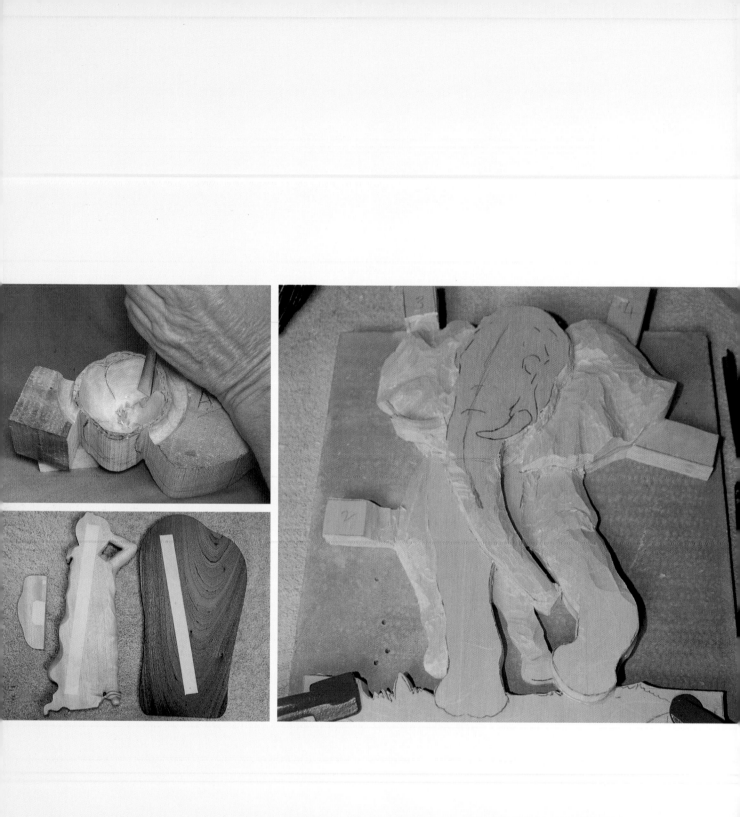

Further projects

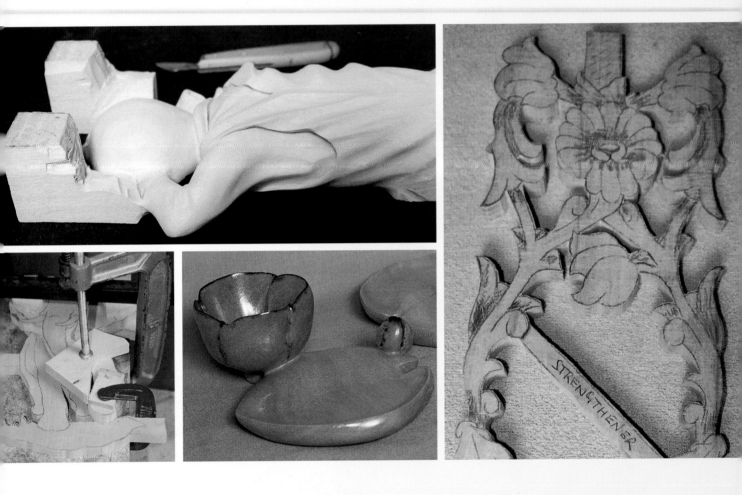

9 Naughty child

TIMBER

Carving: basswood (American lime), 8 x 15in (203 x 381mm) x 2in (50mm) thick

Backing: red cedar, 7¹/₂ x 14¹/₂in (190 x 368mm) x ¹/₂in (12mm) thick, or any size larger than the figure

I find basswood excellent to carve; it is perhaps not quite as tight-grained as European lime, and it is a little denser, but also less likely to splinter. It can be left chisel-finished or sanded.

True red cedar is a pleasure to use, either for a backing or to carve with. Often sold as 'red cedar', however, is plantation cedar, which is extremely soft and very furry, making it difficult to obtain a good finish.

This project is designed as an introduction to a simple figure study, with the added challenge of carving cloth folds. The reaction of the material where it touches the body and the way the movement of the body reacts against the material are one of the major factors in this project.

The clay model

Make a model of the design the same thickness as the carving timber, and etch the details of the drawing into it with a skewer.

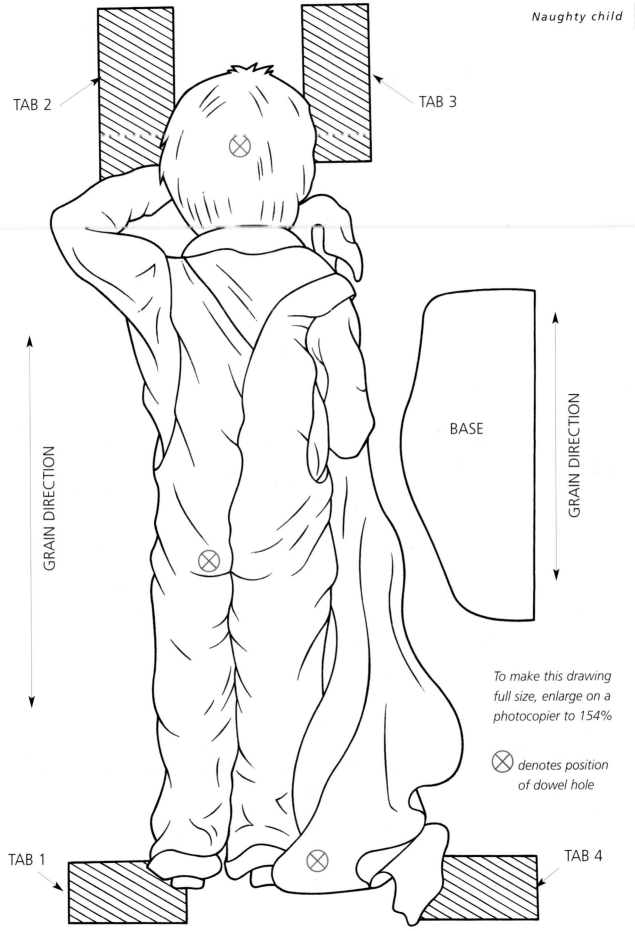

TAB 2

TAB 3

GRAIN DIRECTION

BASE

GRAIN DIRECTION

*To make this drawing
full size, enlarge on a
photocopier to 154%*

⊗ *denotes position
of dowel hole*

TAB 1

TAB 4

Try imagining a child in this position, or stand like this yourself to see where your feet are situated and how the buttocks stick out. There are only two ways to stand like this: either with the bottom stuck out or with the tummy pushed against the wall and the bottom in. The first option has been chosen here.

The overalls will pull against the cheeks of the bottom as the left arm is raised, and the buttocks will stick out the furthest from the body. The blanket sweeps from close to the wall to swell out against the leg and around behind the right foot.

Lower the left arm so that it slopes from shoulder to elbow, then from elbow to wrist.

The right shoulder is now lowered and rounded; because the shoulder is shown dropped, the shoulder strap of the overalls has slipped down. Shape the top half of the overalls, setting in the folds.

Lower the blanket to slope from under the right elbow to the hip. Lower the right arm where it is tucked against the body.

Leave the head slightly oversize to allow the hair to be cut in; the collar can also be fitted into the neck.

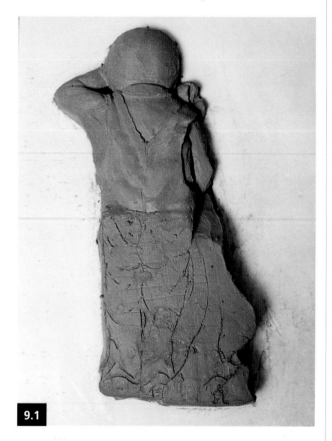

9.1

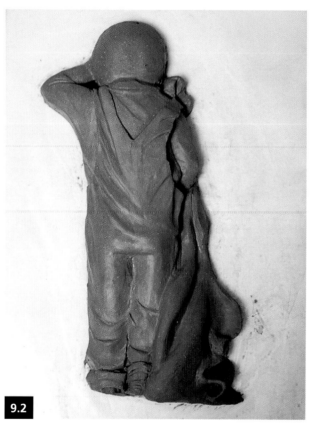

9.2

9.1 Cut the head back to 1³/₈in (35mm) thick, keeping it level for the moment.

Reduce the top section of the blanket to 1in (25mm) thick.

Make a mark at halfway up (at the small of the back), and from this mark to the collar reduce the thickness of the clay by ¹/₂in (12mm), leaving a step for the collar.

Round the head slightly, taking the clay from the edges but not reducing the thickness in the middle.

9.2 Looking at the model, it is apparent that the lower folds of the blanket sweep around and behind the lower part of the right leg. Shaping this part of the blanket first sets the depth for the feet and legs.

Lower the heels by ³/₈in (9mm) and, leaving material for the cuffs, slope up to under the buttocks. Reduce the right heel a further ¹/₈in (3mm) and slope in the same way.

Set the blanket so that it curls slightly around the right lower leg.

Remove clay from under the buttocks and between the legs at the crutch. Shape the bottom, then work up towards the small of the back.

With the buttocks completed, it should be clear what adjustments are required to shape the model and the clothing. Set in the folds in the clothing: the drag will be from the left arm, since this arm is high and the right shoulder dropped.

Clean up the legs of the overalls and allow for the cuffs, remembering to leave material for the folds.

The clay head is left oversize so that when cutting the timber it will not be made too small; the hair still has to be cut into it.

The perspective has now been sorted out and allowances have been made for the folds in the clothing. If any adjustments are needed they are now marked on the pattern and the timber cut.

Carving the figure

All measurements are to be taken from the model, so make any adjustments needed to the model before starting on the wood. We are using the same method to test the depths of the clay and relate that thickness to the timber as we did with the other projects.

Cut the three dowel holes in the back of the carving and make the template as before.

9.3 Use the 8/7 and 9/10 to cut a trench in tabs 2 and 3 for access to the head and left arm. Stab-cut along the pencil lines so the shape is not lost.

Our aim in this carving is to rough out the whole of the timber model and then go back to refine it and work on the details.

Stab-cut the collar and shoulder, and use the 9/10 to reduce the head and the tip of the blanket to the same depth as the model; then level these areas with the fishtail.

Use the V-tool to set in the straps and the V in the back of the overalls, leaving plenty of timber to work on later.

9.4 Lower the surface of the left arm, sloping from shoulder to elbow, then from elbow to wrist. Remove waste from the V-shape below the collar and cut the right arm in.

Use the V-tool to cut in the sides of the overalls and to plan the folds in the cloth; use the 8/7 for the softer folds.

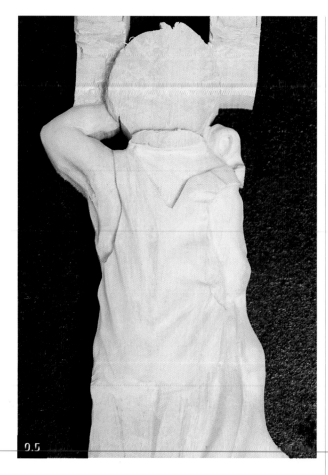

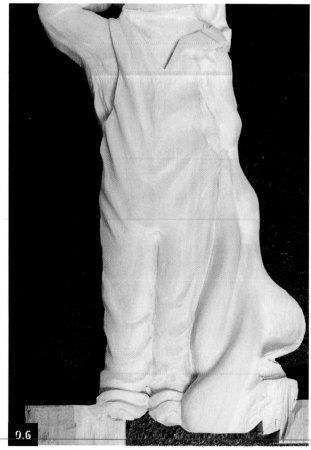

9.5 Sand all over with 180 grit to give a clearer picture of the general effect.

9.6 Stab-cut to set in the cuffs, and work the folds into the trouser legs. The form of the upper legs should be visible where the material is pulled against them. The left side has pulled higher, due to the raising of the left arm. The right side is baggier because the shoulder strap has slipped down, but still pulls against the buttocks.

Cut the groove between the legs with the V-tool and set in the shape of the legs and the folds. The fishtail can also be used to deepen the cleft between the legs; it can be used on either the inside or outside of the blade.

Use the fishtail to set the clearance between the blanket and the right leg, keeping a nice sweep on the folds of material. Gouge the main folds in the blanket, but leave the tight folds on the lower right until the finer details are cut in later. Sand over with 180 grit.

Any changes to the general shape can be done at this point before starting on the final details.

9.7

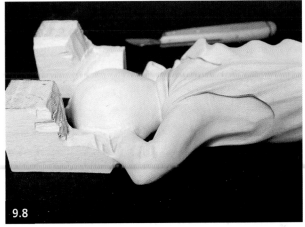

9.8

9.8 If you are satisfied with the shape and contours of the upper area, then undercutting may begin, on the upper torso only. Where access is required, the project may be turned upside down and held securely by the tabs without any risk of damage to the carving.

Start at the area below the left arm; shape the loose folds of the overalls from just above the waist, leaving a space between them and the shirt. All shapes and folds should follow the curve of the body towards the front in a gentle sweep.

Undercut the shirtsleeve and arm up to tab 2 without removing the tab, shape and undercut the inside of the arm. Undercut the front of the overalls where they pull to the front of the chest, keeping the flow of the wrinkles.

Check the thickness of the shoulder strap, lower it to its finished shape and undercut. This strap is narrower than the other, because it has creased as it has been pulled up. The strap is undercut only a small amount – more where deep folds occur.

Use the carving knife as much as possible when undercutting to get the cleanest result; the corner of the fishtail can also be used to good effect, without leaving ugly marks or gouges. At times there is no choice but to use the 3/5 or 5/3 chisel and then sand any tool marks from the timber.

When using the knife, lay the blade as close as possible to the contour of the main timber and draw it slowly along. Raise the blade and cut downwards, following the contours as you draw it towards you,

9.7 Remove the corners from the head block with the 9/10 gouge and smooth over with the fishtail, without lowering the depth. Deepen the trenches in the tabs as needed, but do not remove them yet.

Reduce the collar thickness and work across the back and shoulder area to make it match the head. Use the 8/7 gouge to cut the groove at the nape of the neck, then the 3/5 and sandpaper rolled into a tight tube to soften the contours.

Shave the collar a little at a time with the fishtail; using it upside down leaves a rounded cut. Mark the shape in pencil before cutting.

Standing the carving up vertically and stepping back from it now and then puts the eye in better perspective for viewing the general appearance, and faults are easier to see. Areas that need cutting are marked with soft pencil before clamping down again.

Start rounding the back of the head with either gouge, then smooth off with the fishtail and continue to refine the upper area of blanket, collar, arms. Reduce the thickness of the shoulder straps to suit the new levels and make them fit. Sand all with 180 or 240 grit.

very much in the same way as it was used to undercut the leaves in earlier projects.

When undercutting the folds, make the lower cut first with the knife and then use either the 3/5 or the 5/3 from above to cut down at the required angle; then sand.

Leave the hair until we return to remove the tabs.

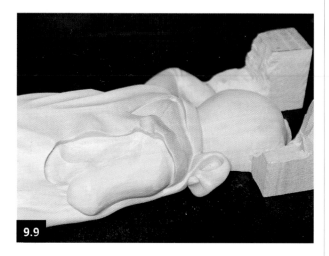

9.9

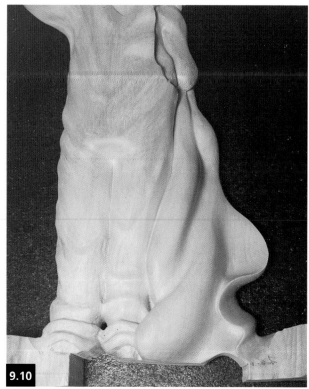

9.10

9.9 On the right side, clean up and shape the tip of the blanket, and finish the blanket folds and right arm where they meet.

Use the 8/7 gouge to shape the blanket folds. To sand the narrow space between blanket and shoulder, fold a long strip of sandpaper and use a sawing motion, taking care not to break off the fragile end.

The right arm and shoulder are tucked against the body and the blanket, so they are not very visible. Suggesting the folds and shape is sufficient, providing some definition is shown.

9.10 Continue to work down the right side, shaping both the right leg and the blanket, cleaning any marks and clarifying details. Sand the blanket, but leave the very lowest right-hand folds until later.

Undercut the buttocks slightly and sand. Deepen the valley between the legs if required. Remove the waste between the legs by using the carving knife or the tip of the fishtail; turn the fishtail to cut with either the left or right edge of the tip as needed.

The sharp fold or crease between the right leg and the blanket is cut in the same manner as between the legs. The inside curve of the fishtail (used upside down) is perfect to keep the sweep of the blanket while removing waste. The left tip of the fishtail, or the carving knife, can then be used to cut down alongside the trouser leg to complete the shape.

If using the carving knife to cut the deep recesses between legs and blanket, then cant the knife at a slight angle. Repeat the cut, angling the knife the opposite way.

Mark the contours of the blanket folds lightly in pencil; they can be altered to suit your own tastes very simply as the shape emerges. Use the 9/10 and

8/7 gouges to get nice sweeps into the outside curves of the folds; the fishtail is useful to even up the surface.

For the inside curve of the tight folds at the bottom, stab-cut the boundary line, then use the 5/3, 3/5 or 8/7 to remove the waste a little at a time. Finish by sanding.

The deep gap between the lower right leg and the blanket is cut using the 5/3, a little at a time. When the depth required has been reached, the bottom is then scraped by dragging the chisel back and forth. Smooth with sandpaper rolled into a tight tube.

Set in the trouser cuffs, and drill the space between the ankles using a ⅛in (3mm) drill bit. Complete the shape with the 5/3 chisel, then sand.

The blanket should now project beyond the trouser leg slightly; leave the tab as it is. Cut back the shoe so the heel is below the level of the cuff.

match the area above the waist that was completed earlier. Mark where you think the side seam of the trouser leg should be; this will clarify the thickness of the leg, and where the folds are pulling from.

The waste may then be removed from the front of the leg to provide room for the foot, which will be seen from the side. The whole area is shaved back to the pencil mark shown in the photograph, so that when it is viewed from the side there will be ample depth to show the perspective. The left leg is carved and sanded enough so that no flat spots show from the side profile. The toe will be shaped after the tab has been removed.

9.12 On the left side of the boy's trousers, a pencil mark has been drawn to show where the side seam lies; the carving knife is then drawn down along this mark to cut the seam. Notice that the seam is not straight but tends to follow the wrinkles in the cloth.

Repeat this procedure on the right side, where only part of the seam will be seen because of the folds of the blanket.

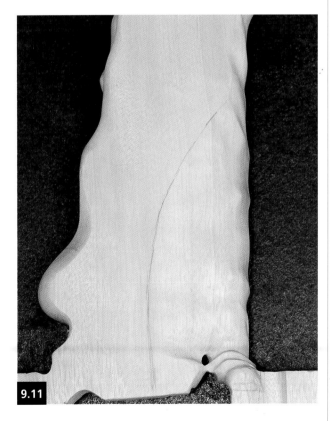

9.11 Shape the outer edge of the left leg before undercutting the front edge; keep the contour of the undercut full and round. Continue to carve in the wrinkles round the side of the cloth, and work it to

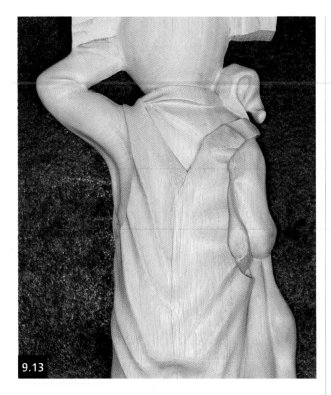

9.13

9.14

9.13 Lightly pencil in the back seam before cutting in the same manner as for the side seams. Note that the top of the seam leans to the right where the strap falls from the shoulder; the seam also follows the humps in the cloth. Cut it by drawing the carving knife firmly along the pencil mark, preferably all in one stroke.

Now check over the entire project in case blemishes have been missed, and sand where required.

9.14 Using the 8/7 gouge and only making shallow cuts, pare away tab 2 a little at a time, staying outside the line of the carving. Clean up using the fishtail, and finish any adjustments needed to the contour to complete the arm; then sand.

If any marks persist in the neck and collar region, either roll the sandpaper into a tight tube to access them, or fold the sandpaper in half then fold again to form a tight, firm rolled edge.

Leave tab 3; it will be the last to be removed.

There are many ways to show hair, but a simple shaggy style is the easiest and will suit this project. If we give the boy curly hair there will be difficult areas to get into at the sanding stage. Straight, neatly combed hair would not suit this subject, and is also harder to cut.

I recommended practising the style on the clay model (using a kebab stick) before cutting into the wood. This helps to give a clear idea of what you are trying to achieve.

Notice that all the directions of hair fall from the crown of the head. Drawing some directions lightly with the pencil before you start cutting helps you to stay oriented.

Cut a gap in the hair where the left arm meets the head; this will allow the hair to 'open up' and fall around the wrist. Use the 3/5 or 5/3 to give this gap some depth, by leaving a slight bulge above the wrist; lines may be cut into it to suggest hair.

I have used the V-tool to make all the cuts. Some have been only lightly cut in, while others have been cut more heavily. Try not to keep all the cuts straight, but sweep them or cross over them as you please. What we are after is a 'messed-up' look, so try not to be too formal.

When you are satisfied with the general effect, use the carving knife to score many finer hair lines all over the head, leaving the area around tab 3 to be finished later, then sand lightly.

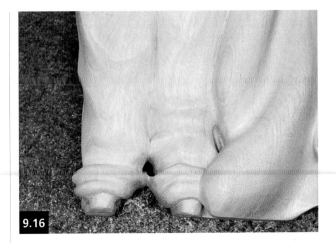

9.16

9.16 Using the 8/7 or the fishtail, gently cut away the bulk of tab 1, leaving enough material to finish the left trouser cuff and shoe.

Continue to shape the cuff on the outer side of the shoe to match up with the front and back. When you are satisfied with the size and shape, finish shaping the boot, which is set back below the level of the cuff.

Before cutting off the waste below the heel, draw a baseline to ensure that it is in line with the right foot and the blanket. Use the bastard file if needed to get this area level, taking care not to damage the tip of the blanket.

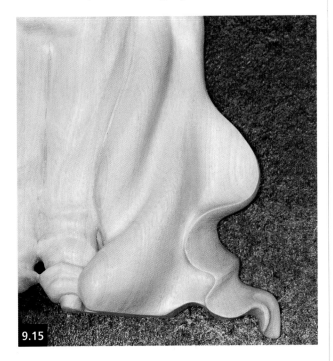

9.15

9.15 Hold the carving by tab 1 and gently cut away the waste from tab 4 until it is the same thickness as the blanket.

Draw the tip of the blanket onto the wood with a pencil. Note how the blanket drops over at the tip; this will allow it to hang over the edge of the base when it is mounted. Shape the remaining wood to fit in with the folds on the blanket and carefully cut away any waste from under the blanket with a fretsaw; then sand.

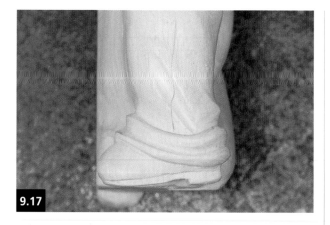

9.17

9.17 Continue the shaping of the foot and shoe, then clean and sand.

Drill two ¹⁄₈in (3mm) holes, one under the centre of the right foot, the other under the centre of the blanket area, for dowelling the boy to the base. Make a template of this area in the usual way.

9.18

Base and backing

9.18 I have used basswood for the base, but a piece of the same material as the backing would also be appropriate. Cut out and sand the base, testing against the feet and blanket to ensure a good fit. Secure the template to the base and drill matching holes for the dowels. Cover the holes with masking tape so polish will not get in; check the base against the carving to make sure the polished area is clear.

The shape I have given for the backing panel is an informal design; if you prefer a different shape, decide now. The backing is planed, cut to shape and sanded all over.

Fit the template of the boy to the backing and drill the matching holes for the dowels. Cover the holes with masking tape to keep out the polish and leave a clean area for the glue.

Brush all three sections of carving with clean, hot tap water and leave overnight to dry, then sand all over with either 0000 steel wool or very fine sandpaper. I applied three coats of oil to the entire project by the 'rubbed' method.

The hanger will not be placed in the centre of the backing this time, because the figure, which is the greatest weight, will be attached off-centre. Place the boy in position on the backing and make a small chalk mark at the top of the backing, in line with his right leg. Remove the boy and turn the backing face down onto a towel. Make a chalk mark at the top, then measure down 1¹⁄₂in (38mm) and mark with a pencil. Wipe off the chalk mark and attach one flap hanger on the back at the pencil mark.

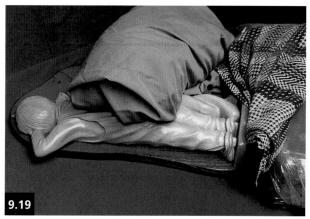

9.19

9.19 Strip off the masking tape from the various pieces and check that there are no lumps or hard drops of polish on the surfaces that are to be glued. Carefully remove any hardened drips that you find with the fishtail.

Cut the dowels to length and fit them into the carving without glue to check that all the segments still align perfectly. When satisfied, apply glue and fix the boy to the backing. Check the alignment of the base plate, apply glue and allow all three parts to set for 24 hours with cloth and weights to keep them firmly together.

10 Matriarch

TIMBER

Carving: jelutong, 20¹/₂ x 10in
(520 x 254mm) depending on layout
of pattern, 1in (25mm) thick

Backing: pine, 25⁵/₈ x 10¹/₄in
(650 x 260mm), ⁵/₈in (16mm) thick

This project is an example of working two
levels of timber; this gives more depth to
the perspective, while retaining the detail.

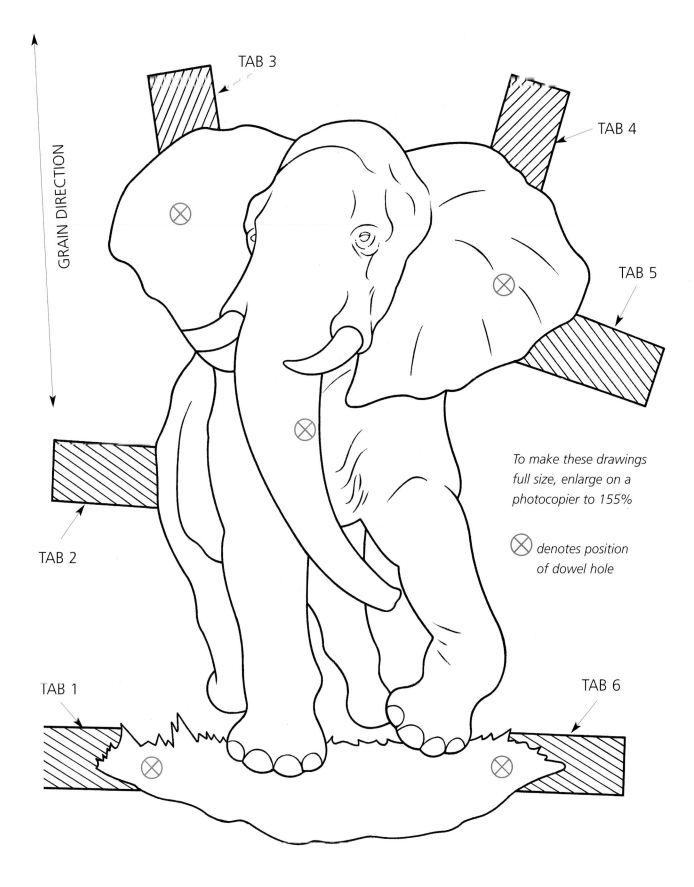

GRAIN DIRECTION

TAB 3

TAB 4

TAB 5

TAB 2

*To make these drawings
full size, enlarge on a
photocopier to 155%*

⊗ *denotes position
of dowel hole*

TAB 1

TAB 6

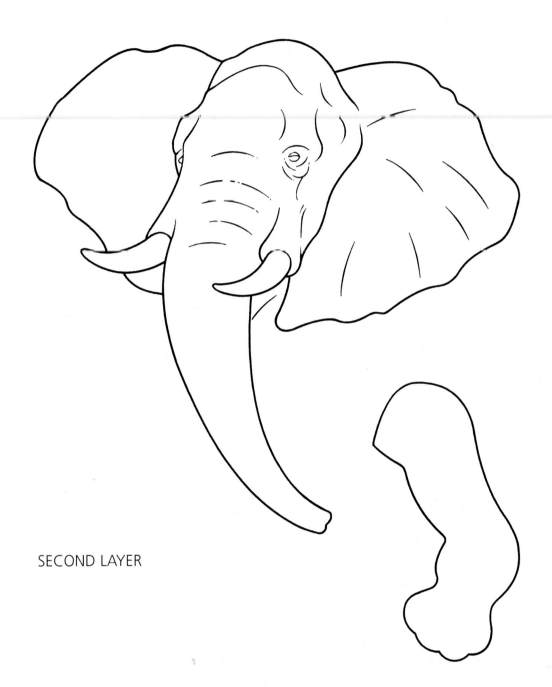

SECOND LAYER

10.1

10.1 The clock that will be incorporated in this project is a sealed-unit type and is fitted by simply pushing into a recess.

10.2

Preparing the timber

10.2 Both ends of the pine shown here have been angled and random-cut after the board was planed. The board has been chamfered down using the fishtail at each end, then sanded. A plain rectangular background may be used if you prefer, of a size to suit your own tastes.

The ends have had black stain at half-strength rubbed into them; they were then sanded, and finally darkened where needed with full-strength stain. Alternatively, they could be burnt with a torch or flame to give a similar result. Leave the oiling of the backing until later.

Cut a hole to suit your clock; mine needed to be 2¼in (58mm) in diameter. This can be cut with a hole saw if you have one, or by marking the circle, drilling a starter hole and then cutting out with a scrollsaw or fretsaw.

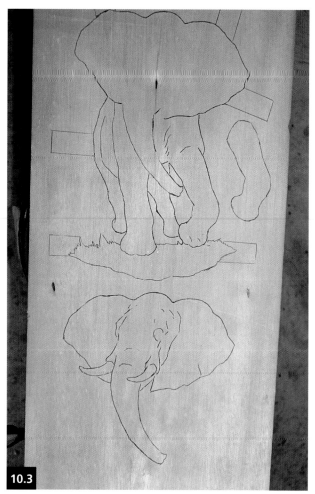

10.3

10.3 Plane the plank on both sides and ensure it is flat. Lay out the design as shown, making sure that the grain in all pieces runs vertically through the pattern. As before, mark the outer waste areas to be tested later. Drill access holes for the saw as necessary, and then cut out the timber sections ready for gluing.

10.4

10.4 Spread the glue on both surfaces and clamp firmly, ensuring that blocks of waste timber are placed under the clamps so as not to crush the carving wood. Leave for 24 hours to set hard. Check that the supporting surface is flat; if it is curved or uneven, the wood will split under the pressure of the clamps. Any distortion will also defeat the purpose of planing the timber first.

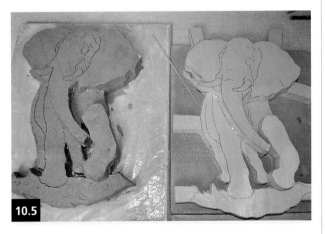

10.5

The clay model

10.5 Make the clay model in three sections:
1 Full elephant body: make in the normal way.
2 Elephant head: make separately on plastic, then peel off and lay on top of the main model.
3 Front leg: make the same way as the extra thickness of head, and lay on top of the right leg.

(As before, 'left' and 'right' are from the viewer's standpoint.)

The timber, glued and ready to carve, is shown next to the finished model.

Spray the model with water and cover with plastic when leaving it overnight.

10.6

10.6 Draw the details on the clay with the skewer to keep all the reference points visible, or prick holes through the paper before removing it.

Slope from behind the left front leg at the shoulder to the rump, leaving a slight bulge for the belly. Reduce the thickness of the rear legs. The left rear foot is lifted, with toes pointing down; round it to form the thickness of the foot. The right rear foot is forward, so must be left thicker at the front, sloping back to the thigh.

Scrape clay from the sides of the head to leave a trough between head and ears.

Cut the clay of the right front leg so that it angles back to the body. It will have a groove where the leg bends at the armpit, and should slope from here to the chest. Lower the clay above the shoulder so that it slopes back into the neck under the ear. Cut clay away from the ankle of the front right foot and shape the foot.

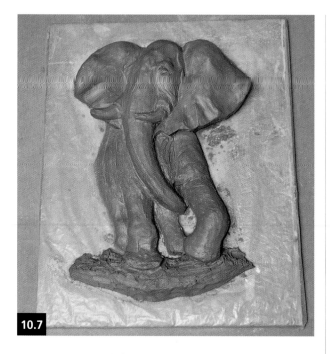

10.7

10.7 Lower the left ear by ¹⁄₄in (6mm) all over to help give the appearance of the head being turned. Scoop out the inner area near the head, and cut the tip right down to the backing board in a slope. Form dips in the soft, flexible parts of the outer ear, and lower the ear behind the tusk.

The left side of the head and trunk can be seen to angle back towards the left ear; the eye is only partly visible, due to the turn of the head.

Carve some of the clay away from the root of the tusk and shape towards the tip, removing only a small amount from the thickness of the tip.

The top of the head should angle back, and there should also be a noticeable dip in the brow.

Gouge a hollow in the right ear, close to the head; this should cut in sharply at the brow. Dips are cut out with a spoon to emphasize the fullness of the ear, while the tip is left high so that it appears to swing forwards.

The right side of the head is now shaped. Slope and round the dome of the head to match the other side, keeping a dip at the brow.

Cut from the trunk towards the tusk, and lower the trunk towards the tip to make it look as if it is curling under. Remove clay from the right side of the trunk to shape it.

Shape around the eye, leaving some fullness where skin tends to bag at the root of the tusk. Carefully scrape clay from the root of the tusk to round it, but leave the tip alone.

Do not try to be exact about details on the clay model, as long as the general shape and contour fit where they are meant to be. It is far more important to get the perspective correct – the details will not make it look right if the perspective is wrong.

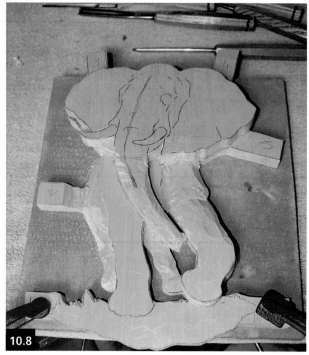

10.8

Carving the figure

10.8 Drill the ¹⁄₄in (6mm) holes for the dowels before starting the carving. Five holes are needed: one in each ear, one in the centre at the point of thickest depth, and one each end of the ground area, again at the thickest place. Make a template in the usual manner, for placement on the backing.

The thickness of the model may be tested with a skewer and transferred to the timber as before.

Cut a trench in tab 2. (Depending on the timber being used, you may find that you will not require tabs 2 and 5, but it is better to have them than to need them.) Use the knife to cut along the left shoulder right down to the foot; also cut the right side of the same leg.

Lower the wood behind the shoulder with the fishtail and slope it down to the backboard, allowing a bulge for the belly. Shape the left leg as for the clay (using the 9/10), allowing enough timber for the toe to come forward. The side of the leg will be angled using the fishtail.

Use the 8/7 and the fishtail to shape the right hind leg; refer to the model to keep the shape and thickness in mind.

Pare back the right front leg with the fishtail, using the V-tool to cut the groove where the leg joins the body. Shave the side of the shoulder and the slope of the trunk with the fishtail.

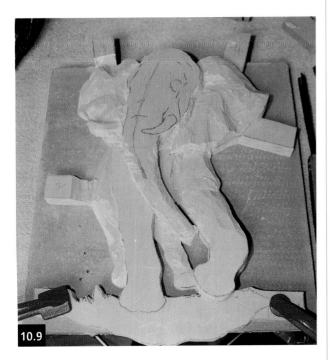

10.9 Note the pencilled centre line on the head: this is the highest part of the carving, and also indicates the direction in which the elephant is facing.

Reduce the thickness of the left ear by 1/4in (6mm); turn the work and hold it by tabs 3 and 4 if required.

Cut carefully along the left side of the head, either with the knife or by stab-cutting with the fishtail. Cut the hollow in the ear next to the head, shape the outer ear and use the knife to cut along the tusk. Remove wood from next to the tusk, lower the tip of the tusk and slope it in to the head in a curve; do not undercut at this stage.

Cut along the right side of the head and lower the surface to get the required profile as in the model. with the appropriate depth at the division of the head and ear. Leave the tip of the ear high, and cut wood away from the tip to make it curl forwards.

Reduce the size of the lip and angle it back towards the tusk.

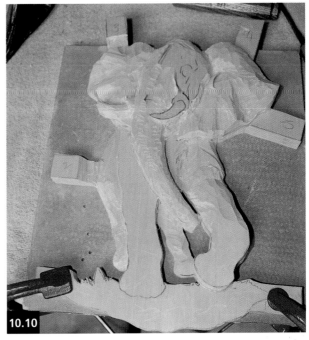

10.10 Note how the 9/10 gouge has been used to angle the front, flattish part of the trunk across the centre line. A slight cant to the left has been formed by paring wood from the outer left edge, so as to turn the trunk away and give it the slightly flat face that trunks have. The top front of the head is left untouched at this stage. Cut carefully along the inner tusk line, and slope the wood from the edge of the 'flat' of the trunk to a hollow at the root of the tusk; use the 3/5 or 8/7 gouge for this.

Cut the lower tusk line and use the 8/7 to pare the trunk down to the mouth. Use the 3/5 to clean up near the tusk.

Use the fishtail to slope the right side at the top of the head.

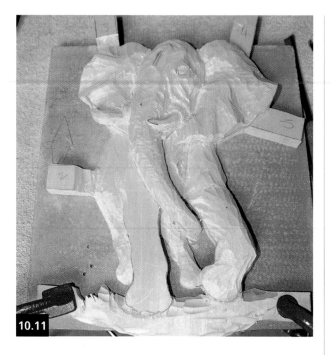

10.11

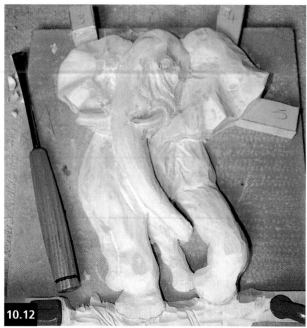

10.12

10.11 Use the 9/10 gouge to form the dip in the head between eye and ear; use the same tool to cut the dip in the top front of the skull above the centre-line mark.

Stab-cut with the 3/5 along the crease where a fold of skin lies on the root of the tusk, and gently pare the tusk down to the fleshy area.

Use the 3/5 or 5/3 to stab-cut the pencil mark at the eye position, then carefully remove 1/8in (3mm) of depth from the eye itself. Either gouge may be used to cut the hollow under the eye, which must be angled down to the tusk. The V-tool is used to cut the tight 'sags' in the skin that run from the face and eye down to the tusk.

Pare more wood away from the trunk from the chest level to the tip to give it more of a curl.

Bevel the front edge of the ground area by cutting scoops out of it with the 9/10 gouge. This area is meant to be left rough, so cut the front edge only.

10.12 Leaving the toe alone for the moment, shape the left front knee by reducing the wood around it. Take care, as only small amounts need to be removed to give the requisite dip or hollow. Shape the inside of the leg from knee to armpit with the fishtail. Slope the top of the leg the same way on the outside. Lower the belly more if necessary to get the required depth of the inside leg at the top.

Check the height from shoulder to rump: it should slope back and be almost flat at the top to give the right perspective.

Lower the timber under the knee and above the foot, and shape to give a rounded look, sloping to the toe area.

Shape the right front leg back towards the body to the point where chest and body meet, deepening the groove where the leg joins. Lower the junction between shoulder and chest, and cut 'sags' or folds in the skin with the V-tool. Round the knee and pare the timber back so that the foot turns under more; use the 9/10 to keep the ankle rounded.

Carefully remove tab 2.

Before doing any undercutting, sand the whole project with coarse and then medium sandpaper. It will be plain to see any areas that still require work after sanding has been completed.

10.13

10.13 Because the tabs are only as thick as the lower level of timber, this design cannot be turned over for undercutting. Instead, turn it around and hold it by tabs 1 and 3, trench-cutting tab 3 just deeply enough to give some access while you partly undercut that area.

Starting with the left ear, slowly undercut the outer edges, shaping all down to the backing board only enough so that the undercut area will not show from the front; sand as you go.

Clean up the trench where head and ear meet; this should be a sharp angle, free of chisel marks or fluff.

Turn the design, clean up around the eye and recut to keep the sharpness.

Slowly undercut the tusk and lower lip with either 3/5 or 5/3, and sand.

Work along the right side of the trunk, undercutting as you go. Trim the trunk to length by undercutting the tip and cutting a recess in it with the 8/7.

Undercut both sides of the right leg from the shoulder forwards, finishing the rounding process.

Turn the design, undercut the right ear and remove tab 5. Slightly undercut the head where it meets the ear, and finish the eye.

Clean up around the root of the tusk and slowly undercut the tusk and the lower part of the ear against the body.

Continue along the trunk, undercutting to the tip.

The left front leg needs to be slightly undercut all the way down to the foot. Check to see if the junction of belly and rear leg requires deepening.

Mark the toes in lightly with pencil before cutting. S-cut around the pencil line using the 3/5, then pare back to this cut so that the toenail is rounded. Elephant toenails are almost the same as human thumbnails with a square-cut nail.

Using the 8/7 and working from front to rear, make short, choppy angled cuts in the ground area. Completely remove tabs 1 and 6 to blend in with the foreground, as shown in the photograph. The last two tabs, 3 and 4, are carefully pared away a little at a time and the adjoining areas sanded.

Wet the whole carving to raise the grain; when dry, sand all over.

Lightly mark with pencil the direction of wrinkles and sags on the trunk before cutting them – if the angle is wrong, the whole project will be spoiled.

Use the V-tool to cut the heavier grooves in the trunk and the body; where slightly lighter grooves are wanted, drag the V-tool instead of pushing it. Finer lines can be achieved by dragging a nail or similar tool, as described for leaf veins on page 31. Extra-thin lines, as seen on the rump and belly, are cut using the carving knife. Finish cutting and marking the wrinkles all over, and lightly sand with fine paper.

Finishing and assembly

Before staining, the tusks and toenails were protected with one coat of Danish oil and allowed to dry. This is to stop the stain from colouring these areas, and to allow the natural colour of the wood to show.

Try the stain on offcuts first. For my carving I used Proof Tint Black, diluted to half-strength with thinner.

I allowed this to dry, then rubbed it back with more thinner on a cloth. One more coat of the same mix was applied to the ears only and rubbed back with a cloth on the high areas. I then allowed the whole project to dry before oiling with two coats of Danish oil.

Remove the clock and the carving and, using an extremely thin wash of black, block in the rough shape of the furthest elephant, keeping in mind that the further away they are, the smaller they appear. The next elephant is done with a slightly darker wash and is also bigger; then do another, darker and larger again. Work some grasses in the same manner, having the darkest shadows near the front.

Allow to dry, and then coat with two coats of varnish, or until it suits your preferences.

Before attaching the carving, place the backing face down on a soft cloth and affix two triangular hangers and a suitable length of picture wire.

Fix the carving with dowels in the usual manner, and leave to set under weights for 24 hours.

10.14

10.14 Some shading has been done on the background to suggest the herd of elephants that are following; if you do not wish to add them, just oil the backing board.

Fit the clock into the hole and place the Matriarch loose onto the backing. Move her until the position is most suitable to your tastes, then make a chalk mark at the baseline where her feet touch the ground.

11 Water poppies

TIMBER

Carving: basswood, 10 x 8¼in

(254 x 210mm), 2in (50mm) thick (or can be

cut from two pieces of timber – see drawing)

Base: walnut, 11in (280mm) diameter,

1in (25mm) thick

Stand: any timber, 3in (76mm) diameter,

2in (50mm) thick

Basswood was chosen for this carving not just because of its paleness. I required a timber that would be strong and stable, without tearing when cutting across the grain. As you can see in the drawing on page 123, the grain runs horizontally through the work, so, while the leaves have their grain lengthwise, the poppies themselves will be cut fairly thin in cross grain. Many other timbers would not lend themselves to this approach: they would splinter and break away, or crumble when being handled during sanding. However, others such as camphor laurel could have been used with the same confidence as basswood.

I used walnut for the base for two reasons: its depth of colour, for contrast with the carving, and its weight, which gives stability to the carving when finished. The stand can be made from any timber, but it is better if this is also fairly dense.

Water poppies *(Hydrocleys nymphoides)* are a deciduous or semi-evergreen perennial deep-water plant with poppy-like flowers held above the floating foliage. They are a pale yellow with red-brown stamens. (I have taken a little licence in adding some colour to the rims of the flowers.) They were chosen for this project to show a different method of carving the shape and contour out of a set block of wood.

11.2

Stand

11.2 Use any dark timber that matches your base or that can be stained to match. Cut it into a 3in (76mm) circle, using the file to even the outer edge before sanding. Wet to raise the grain and sand again before staining if required.

11.1

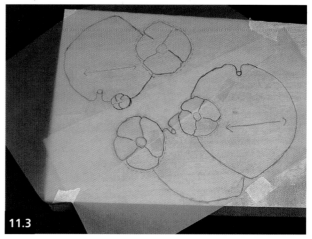
11.3

Walnut base

11.1 Plane the board and mark the circle with a compass – or you could use a dinner plate or similar as a template. Cut the walnut out on a bandsaw, or cut by hand as previously described (page 51).

After sanding, mark a line all the way around the underside 1/2in (12mm) in, and bevel from this mark to the opposite edge. Use any gouge to remove the bulk of the waste; when nearing completion, use the fishtail, then finish off with the bastard file as in the Foliage project.

11.3 Before cutting the timber for the flowers, draw the design onto tracing paper and lay it over the base timber. The grain will be clearly visible through the tracing paper, making it simple to choose where you wish to position the flowers to enhance the carving. Marking the grain direction on the tracing will help you in positioning the design on the wood.

Use masking tape to hold the tracing in position, then slide the carbon paper under it – this way the design will not move.

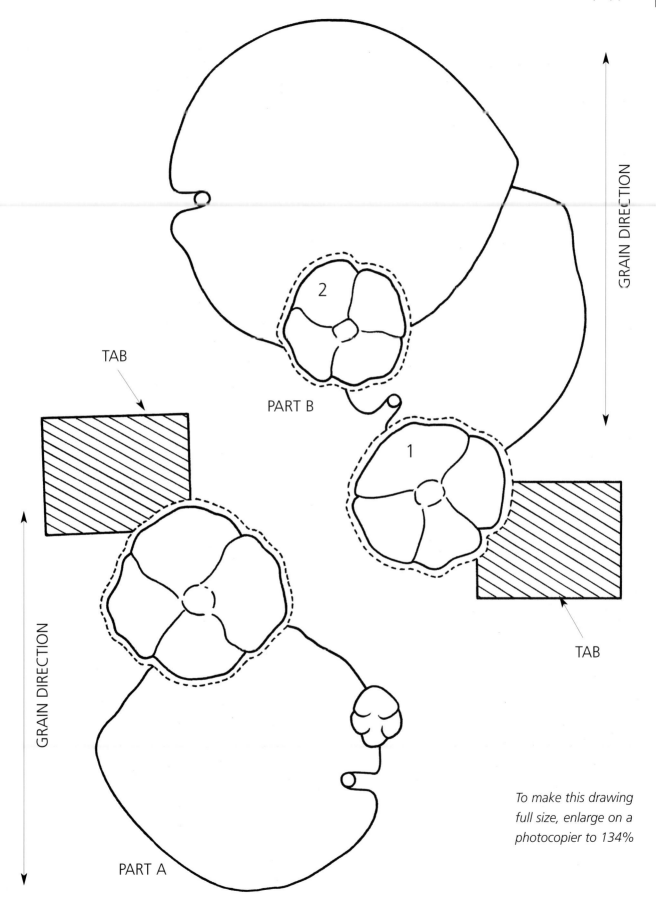

GRAIN DIRECTION

PART B

TAB

1

TAB

GRAIN DIRECTION

PART A

To make this drawing full size, enlarge on a photocopier to 134%

Notice the dotted lines round the outside of the flowers: the timber should be cut to this line. Cut as normal on the solid line for the leaves.

For ease of working it is best to cut A and B as two separate pieces; this will also give you more flexibility in fitting the design on the timber.

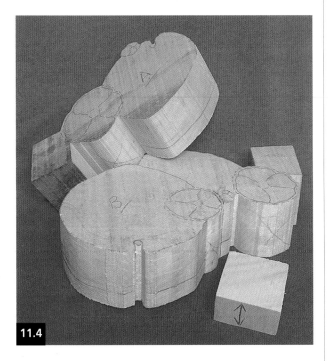

11.4

11.4 Mark a line ½in (12mm) from the bottom on both sections A and B. Notice the small pieces with the grain running vertically that have been saved from the offcuts: these will later be used to make the stamens.

This time there is no point in making a clay model, as the shape is very simple and we will be working downwards all the time. The lily pads or leaves are almost flat, and the poppies are a simple cup shape.

The difference, however, is that this time the centre of each flower is completely shaped before the outside is cut. Leaving the outer timber intact gives support and strength to the flower while it is being worked; the outer is then shaped a little at a time to conform to the inner shape.

Carving part A

Please note that in some pictures the clamps have been removed to give a clearer view for photography.

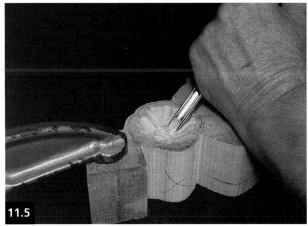

11.5

11.5 Hold the work with a G-cramp anywhere except on a flower or bud. Working from the outer edge of the flower, cut in towards the centre with the 9/10 or 8/7 gouge. Take only small cuts. Work your way around the whole area, cutting the centre deeper each time around but staying well within the pencil line at the rim. Make sure that the inside of the flower wall is not straight – a curved inner wall like the inside of a teacup is the shape that is required. Take care not to lean on the top edge of the carving, as it may crumble or break. If the timber tends to tear, use the 8/7 and make thinner cuts. You will get better results if your gouges are sharpened with a reasonably steep bevel – a shallow bevel would cause the tool to dig in.

11.6

11.6 The cavity does not have to be symmetrical, but you can see that ridges have been left to form the edges of the petals. Measure the depth of the recess regularly so that you do not cut too deep.

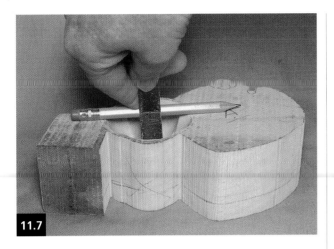

11.7

11.7 A small ruler and a pencil (or similar) laid across the top of the recess can be used to gauge the depth. Use the 9/10 to scrape the base at the bottom of the hollow to make a reasonably flat surface for the stamen to sit on.

11.9

11.9 With the 8/7 or the 9/10, cut a trench ¼in (6mm) deep outside the dotted line to allow access to the rim. Mark in pencil where the petal edges are on the inside of the flower, noting that if the left edge of a particular petal is on the inside then the right edge of that petal will be on the outside, because they overlap. Also mark a slight curve in the top edge, and where the petals lie on the outside of the flower.

11.8

11.8 Sand the inside with 180 and 240 grit, enough so that the shape can be seen; but don't worry about some undulations in the form. It helps if the sandpaper is wrapped around a chopstick or similar; this gives more reach and saves the wear on the fingers while allowing more pressure to be applied.

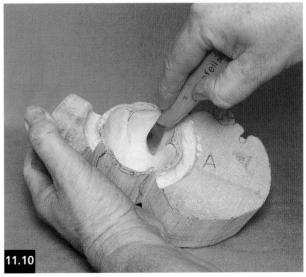

11.10

11.10 Use the carving knife held at an angle to cut the edges of the petals on the inside. Cutting at an angle allows for a slight undercut when the waste is removed. The cut need not go all the way to the bottom, and should only penetrate the wood to a depth of 1/16in (1.5–2mm) or a fraction more. If it is cut too heavily, it will show through when the outside profile is shaped.

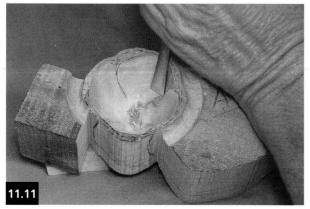

11.11

11.11 Using the corner of the fishtail, gently cut away the timber to the left of the knife-cut line; this will leave a small undercut on the petal edges. Sand clean, working through the grades of sandpaper. Pressure can be applied while the walls of the flower are supported by the waste; once this has been cut away they will be very fragile.

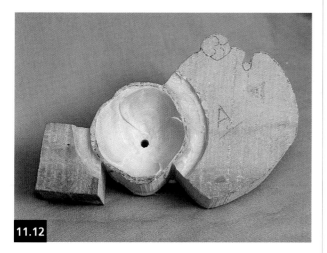

11.12

11.12 Mark the centre of the inside and drill a 1/4in (6mm) hole all the way through the base. This serves both for dowelling the flower to the base and for fixing the stamens.

11.13

11.13 Cut the leaf and the tab down to the depth of the trench using the fishtail, then recut the trench in the same manner as before. This now leaves the rim of the flower exposed enough for it to be shaped with the inside curve of the fishtail.

Before starting to cut the petals, mark where their edges sit at the top edge of the flower, and where the outer petals overlap. Use the carving knife to cut the separation between the petals on the outer edge.

By working down slowly, cutting each section and sanding as we go, we are working with the strongest section of the timber at all times.

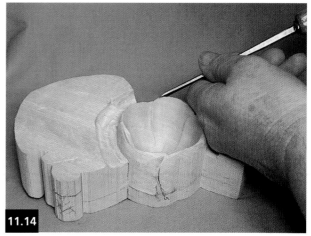

11.14

11.14 The contouring of the outside can now be started. Use the knife to cut in the outer petals, undercutting with the fishtail as before. Use the inner curve of the fishtail to shape the outer edge of the rim. Lower the leaf and the tab to the level of the trench, then recut the trench.

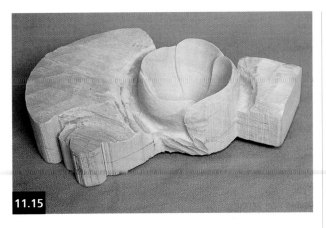

11.15

11.15 Mark the height of the bud on the outside of the timber at 1¼in (32mm) from the bottom. When this depth is reached, draw the bud on the surface of the timber and cut a trench around it so that it won't get cut off by mistake. Continue to shape the outside of the flower as you work down, leaving the bud until later.

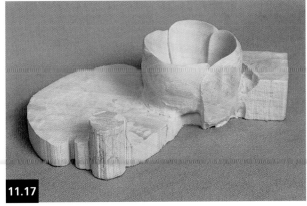

11.17

11.17 When nearing the pencil line which marks the height of the leaf pad, cut away small amounts until the surface is almost flat. Continue to shape the flower and start to undercut the stem area. The bud is left standing, ready to shape.

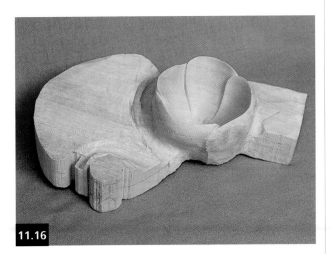

11.16

11.16 By recutting the trenches each time as the level is lowered you minimize the risk of the timber splitting, or the chisel running into the flower. The outside of the poppy is profiled and sanded in stages as you work down.

11.18

11.18 Mark the centre of the leaf, and use the 9/10 to slope the surface towards the centre. With the same chisel cut a groove in the edge opposite the flower to form a raised rim. Shape the bottom edge of the flower, leaving the stem thick around the previously drilled hole.

11.19

11.19 Sand the flower smooth. Note how the leaf dips down where the flower sits on it. The outside edge opposite the poppy has been rounded using the inside of the fishtail. The edge where the poppy sits has been cut lower and undercut, using either the knife or the fishtail and the 3/5. Sand all edges.

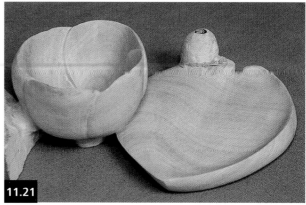

11.21

11.21 Draw a 1/8in (3mm) circle on the top of the bud. With the timber clamped by the tab, gently cut away the corners to form a dome shape. Any chisel may be used, but take only small cuts and do not lean heavily on the bud or strike hard with the mallet, which might snap the bud off.

11.20

11.20 Turn the project over and carefully cut away the waste between the tab and the central hole. Leave a ring around the stem, and finish shaping the bottom of the flower and the undercut edges of the leaf. The work will have to be held in the hand while this is done, so care must be taken with the chisels. Do not remove the tab.

11.22

11.22 Start to shape the bottom edge of the bud where it sits against the leaf, undercutting it with the 3/5 and continuing the downturn of the leaf edge.

11.23

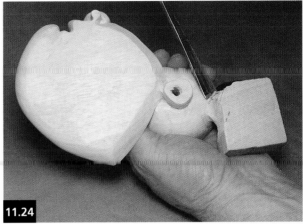

11.24

11.23 Draw the petals onto the bud, and use the knife to cut along the pencil lines at a slight angle so as to leave a small undercut.

Mark in pencil where the stem comes up from the water and is attached to the leaf. Cut the edges away and slope this part down using the 3/5 to form a stem.

When removing wood from the outside of the bud, cut and sand at an angle from left to right so as to put a twist into the shape.

At the top of the bud, where the petals cross over, there is a diamond shape; use the 5/3 to stab-cut along these lines. Remove a small amount of wood to leave a depression about 1/16in (1.5mm) deep.

11.24 Holding the flower carefully, slowly cut away the remains of the tab. Take care that the chisel is not facing your hands as you pare away the remains of the tab. If you have protective gloves, wear them. Sand where necessary, then put part A in a safe place until part B is completed; do not oil yet.

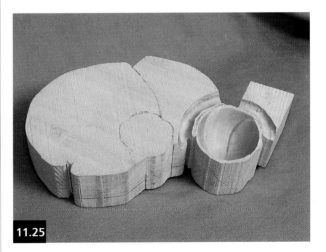

11.25

Part B

11.25 Remove 1/4in (6mm) from the entire face of part B, then redraw the details of the flowers on the timber, both inner and outer lines.

Hollow the larger flower (1) next to the tab in the same manner as was done for part A, shaping and sanding the inside as before and drilling a 1/4in (6mm) hole in the centre. Cut and shape the petals in the same manner as for part A, and then cut a 1/4in (6mm) trench around the flower.

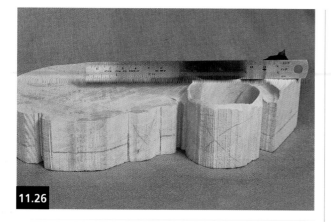

11.26 Shape the top edge of flower 1 next to the tab, and then lower the entire area of the leaves to the level of the trench. This effectively lowers the level of the second flower by 1/4in (6mm). Redraw flower 2.

11.28 Notice that the outsides of the flowers have only been sanded on the upper areas; the lower parts are still rough. Undercutting cannot take place until the shape and contour of the leaves has been set.

I originally drew both edges of the leaves, before deciding which one would lie on top. Eventually the larger, more dominant leaf was chosen to be on top. The centres are then marked and the knife used to separate the two leaves. Cut towards this line from the centre with the fishtail to leave the larger leaf higher than the smaller.

Use the 8/7 to gouge a dip from the centre of the leaf to the stem; there should be no undercutting yet. Cut a depression along the inside of the large leaf, using the 9/10, to form a curl in the leaf as shown in the photograph.

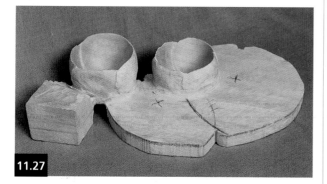

11.27 Continue to shape flower 2 in the same manner as before, while alternately shaping the top rim and outside of flower 1. Continue to cut the trenches as the level is lowered to the pencil mark.

11.29 Note that where the leaves meet, and where the flowers sit, the edges of the leaves are naturally lower than elsewhere.

Continue the shaping of the flowers, and do not start to undercut them until the leaves have been fully shaped.

11.30

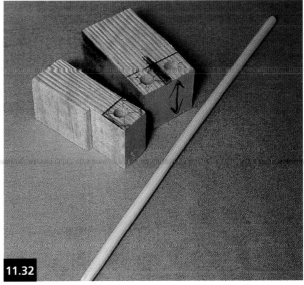

11.32

11.30 Now the poppies can be finished by undercutting where they sit on the pads. The same method is used as before, taking particular care when working between the two flowers. The large leaf can also be undercut and both leaves sanded. Use the inside curve of the fishtail to complete the sweep of the outer undercuts.

All that remains is for the last of the tab to be cut away carefully, as we did with part A.

11.32 To make the stamens, cut a 6in (150mm) length of basswood (or bamboo chopstick) and round it with the file or sandpaper until it is ¼in (6mm) in diameter. Take the small blocks that we cut earlier and mark ½in (12mm) squares on them. Drill a ¼in (6mm) hole in each square.

11.31

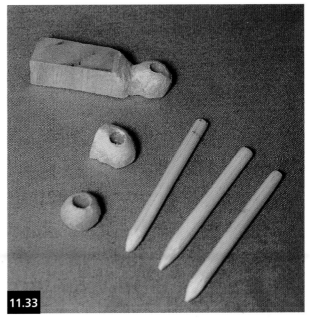

11.33

11.31 Parts A and B are now both complete, and have been wetted, dried and resanded ready for the next step.

11.33 Separate each strip so that there is enough timber to hold with the clamp while the ends are cut into round balls similar to a wooden bead. Cut the dowel into three 2in (50mm) lengths.

Drill a 1/4in (6mm) hole in a piece of waste and insert a piece of dowel so that 1in (25mm) of it stands up clear of the waste timber. Use the fishtail to cut repeatedly down into the dowel until the end has a frayed and ragged look. Repeat with the other two pieces of dowel. These will become the centres of the stamens.

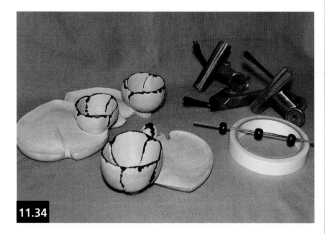

11.34

11.34 All three balls and the three stamen centres, along with the top edges of the flowers, have now had a dark red stain applied to them. I mixed Jarrah with three drops of Black Proof Tint to get the very dark red. Stamens and balls were then dipped into the mix, while a brush was used on the flower edges. To soften the flowers, the colour was then rubbed back with a rag dipped in stain reducer.

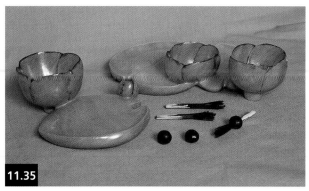

11.35

11.35 Danish oil was applied to all sections, three coats being rubbed on with a rag. The stamens were simply dipped.

Assembly

Drill two 1/4in (6mm) holes in the top of the small circle that we cut for the stand; make a template of these holes and position it on the underside of the large circular base plate. Drill holes in the base plate to match, making sure that you put tape on the drill bit to serve as a depth gauge, so that you do not cut all the way through. Dowel and glue the stand to the base in the usual way.

When the glue has hardened, position the water poppies on top of the base. When you are happy with their placement, take a 3in (76mm) nail, carefully insert it through the hole in one of the flowers and give it a smart tap with the hammer; repeat with the other flower. These indents are the locating marks for the drill. Remove the flowers and drill 1/4in (6mm) holes where marked; check for alignment before gluing.

Place glue into the dowel holes and under the lily pads, slide the stamens through the balls and glue them in place. Apply glue to the stamens and insert them through the poppies into the base, so that the stamens serve also as dowels for the flowers. Place a suitable weight on the pads until the glue is set.

12 Daisy clock

TIMBER

Carving: brown beech,
14 x 6³/4in (355 x 171mm)
(or longer for tabs if
available), ³/4in (18mm) thick

Backing: red cedar,
15 x 7³/4in (381 x 197mm),
¹/2in (12mm) thick

Australian brown beech is a fairly
soft timber, often with golden flecks
throughout that give it a lovely glow.
It can be a bit brittle, and care needs
to be taken if small details are left
where they may get broken off.
It does require sanding, as it tends
to look a little 'woolly' if left
chisel-finished.

The red cedar used as a backing
board was a very old piece rescued
from a demolition yard, previously
having lived its life as a shelf in a
colonial dresser.

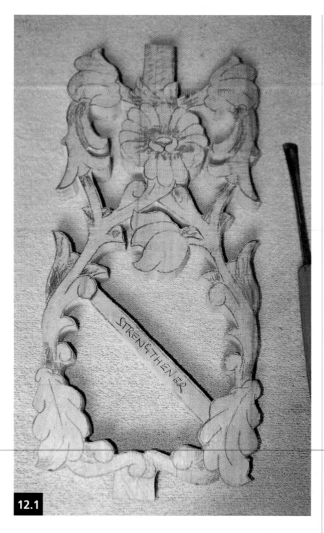

12.1

12.2

12.1 Take note of the strengthening bar shown in the drawing, across where the clock or barometer will fit. Because of the comparatively fragile cutaway design, this will be left in place until all the other carving has been completed.

Notice also that the tabs are a lot smaller than usual. If you wish to make them larger or add more, then please do; however, those shown are enough to hold this design, as the larger corners can also be used for clamping.

Drill holes for access and cut out both outer and inner shapes, leaving the strengthening bar in place.

There will be no model made for this project, as clay would be too flimsy.

There are no fixed rules for this semi-abstract type of design, so it can be useful to mark the lower levels with pencil shading at the start.

Carving

12.2 When clamping directly onto the carving timber, place small blocks of waste under the G-cramps to avoid bruising the timber. Hold at the bottom corners and stab-cut with the fishtail or the 5/3 just above the corner section and on the design lines to separate the upper and lower levels of the design. Cut towards these lines using the fishtail to give long sweeps and curves; the inner curve of the fishtail is perfect here.

Work small areas, doing both sides of the design in turn to keep the balance equal. Sand each section as you work along.

Work to almost halfway, curving the bell-like shapes in a half-round with the fishtail. Remove the top outer edge with the fishtail to give a nicely rounded shape.

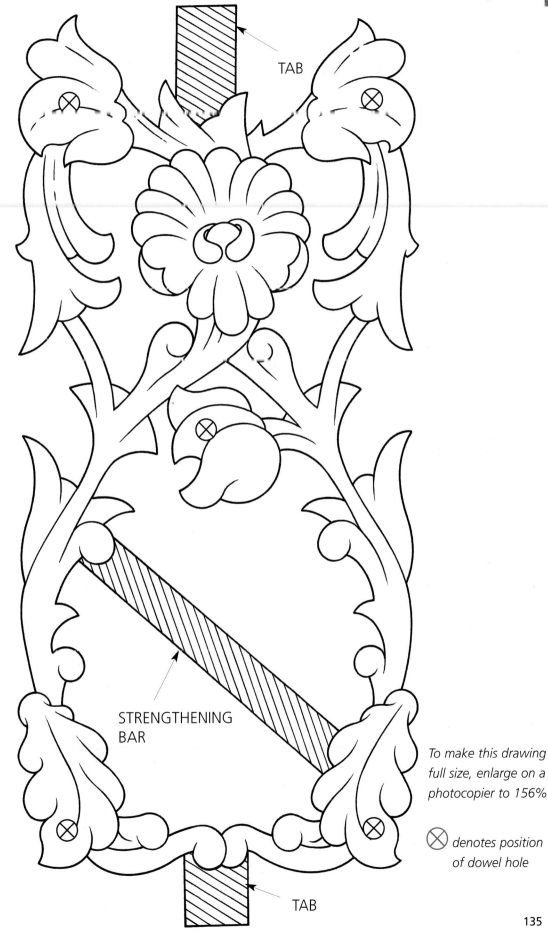

TAB

GRAIN DIRECTION

STRENGTHENING
BAR

*To make this drawing
full size, enlarge on a
photocopier to 156%*

⊗ *denotes position
of dowel hole*

TAB

135

The balls are similar to fern fronds that are just uncurling. By paring timber from the inside of the curl to the stab line with either gouge, and then shaving the outer edge with the fishtail, the roundness will emerge.

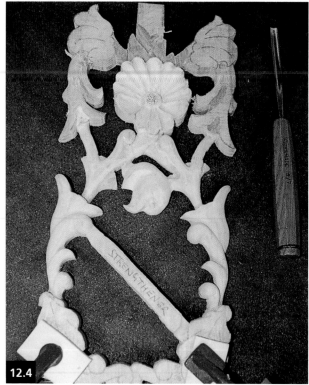

12.3 Stab-cut around the bottom of the daisy with the 5/3 gouge and cut along the stalk lines with the carving knife.

Stab-cut the inner lines of the balls immediately below the daisy, and lower one stalk so that it sits behind the other. Slope the wood to leave the balls higher than the stalks; then sand.

Shape the curling central fan or leaf, using the fullness of the timber to give it contour.

With regard to the bell-shaped flowers which flank the fan, note that their stems need to be thinner than the flaring, trumpet-like parts, so that the latter appear to overlap the stems.

12.4 Stab-cut the centre of the flower with the 3/5, then use the 9/10 gouge to lower the central area only. Use the 8/7 gouge for the tighter, narrower areas nearest the centre.

Stab-cut around the outside of the daisy where the petals touch the outer pattern. Use the carving knife to cut the straight lines separating the fans at the top.

Lower the area outside the daisy and shape these. Cut a trench in the top tab with the 8/7, but do not remove the tab yet.

Starting from the widest petal and using the 8/7 gouge, cut towards the centre of the daisy and work around. Deepen the cuts each time so that the outer edge remains high, with the centre low and the ridges clearly defined.

When the central area has reached its finished height, level off with the fishtail and redraw the details of the stamens before cutting a groove around them with the V-tool. Stab-cut along this groove and gently lower and shape the outer rim of the stamen area. After shaping and sanding, holes can be either drilled with a small bit or made by tapping a small nail repeatedly over the surface; care is needed here.

Clean around the central area with 5/3 and 3/5, undercutting gently the whole central stamen part. Roll sandpaper into a tight tube to sand the petals.

12.5

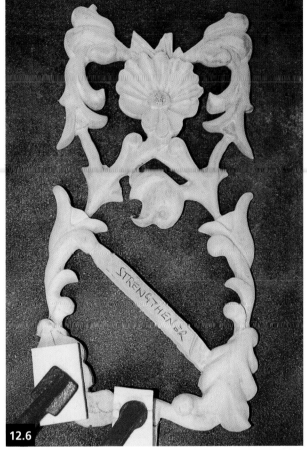

12.6

12.5 Finish shaping the upper side bells, then turn the work and hold by the centre tab while you shape both corner sections.

Shape the small fans above the daisy and below the tab. Turn the work over, undercut all the upper section of the design, and sand all over.

Before removing the tabs, drill holes for the dowels, one in each corner and one in the thickest part of the centre; make a template as usual.

12.6 Turn the work and hold by the bottom corners while you cut away the tab at the top: deepen the trench with the 8/7, clean up with the fishtail and then sand.

Hold the work by the bottom tab and left corner while carving the right corner and adjoining scroll. Use the 8/7 for the grooves; stab-cut the edge of the main flare (the wide, tapering, leaf-like section at the corner), but do not remove the strengthening bar.

Stab the lower balls or fern fronds, and shape them with the inside of the fishtail. Where the leaf-like section at the corner overhangs the stem of the frond, allow it to fold over so as not to leave a sharp edge here. Clean up with the fishtail to soften the curves, then sand.

12.7

12.8

The backing

12.7 Position the work so that it can be held by the strengthening bar and centre tab, then work the left corner to match the right.

Remove the centre clamp, gently carve away the tab and shape to suit.

Slowly carve away a section of each end of the strengthening bar in turn until it is free; use the fishtail to finish off, then sand.

Wet the carving all over with hot tap water and allow the grain to rise. When dry, sand all over, and, when satisfied, apply two coats of Danish oil.

Although this brown beech has a lot of speckles in it, I decided to leave it in its natural colour, which would be complemented by the red cedar backing. This particular old piece of cedar is very dark.

12.8 Plane the backing and cut it to size; file the edges to remove saw marks, then sand it clean. Use the file to round the edges slightly, then sand. Wet to raise the grain, and when dry, sand all over.

Mark a line $5/16$in (8mm) from the edge all the way around the board. Clamp a metal rule to the backing just inside the marked line, and use this as a guide to draw the V-tool down towards yourself to create a depression, stopping short of the corners. A blunt nail may be used instead (as in veining), but make sure that it has had any burrs removed. The corners are finished freehand, so as not to overlap the cuts. Practise on an offcut first.

Oil in the normal manner, and attach the hangers.

Using the template as before, drill the dowel holes in the backing; check their position by placing dowels in the holes and attaching the carving without glue.

Find the centre of the area where the clock or barometer is to fit, and mark and drill a hole of suitable diameter. Lightly sand the edges of the hole, seal with one coat of oil and allow to dry. Now glue the carving to the backing, apply a padded weight and leave for 24 hours to set.

The carving is now ready to be fitted with the clock or barometer of your choice.

Gallery of carvings

CIRCLE OF LIFE
Rosewood, mirror glass

LITTLE OWL
Camphor laurel

REFUGE

Hollow tree: cabbage gum; sugar gliders and leaves: jelutong, stained

WOLF SONG

New Guinea rosewood; base and backing: red ebony

PENDULUM CLOCK
Mulberry

NEZ PERCÉ INDIAN BOY
Mango

URBAN HUNTER

Owl: lime; wall: camphor laurel; leaves and vine: jelutong, stained

SIOUX INDIAN

Camphor laurel, stained

THE ORATOR
Camphor laurel, coloured

Timbers for carving

Listed here are just some of the timbers commonly known and used for carving. This is a personal list, and inevitably the emphasis is on timbers available to me in Australia. There are no rules: if you like to carve it, then it is a good timber for carving.

Beech, Australian brown (pepperwood)	*Cinnamomum laubatii*
Beech, Australian white	*Gmelina dalrympleana/*
	G. fasciculiflora
Beech, European	*Fagus sylvatica*
Beech, Japanese	*Fagus crenata*
Beech, Solomon Island white	*Gmelina salomonensis*
Boxwood, Maracaibo	*Gossypiospermum praecox*
Camphor laurel	*Cinnamomum camphorum*
Camphorwood, Australian	*Cinnamomum oliveri*
Cedar, Australian	*Cedrela toona toonaaustralis*
Cedar, Canadian yellow	*Chamaecyparis nootkatensis*
Cedar, Malaysian red	*Toona sureni/Cedrela serrata*
Cedar, New Guinea	*Cedrela toona/Toona sureni*
Cedar, South American	*Cedrela odorata*
Cheesewood, Australian white	*Wrightia laeuis*
Cherry, American	*Prunus serotina*
Coachwood, Australian	*Ceratopetalum apetalum*
Ebony, Indian black	*Diospyros ebenum*
Ebony, Macassar	*Diospyros* spp.
Huon pine, Australian	*Dacrydium franklinii*
Imbuya/Brazilian walnut	*Phoebe porosa*
Jelutong, Asian	*Dyera costulata*
Kauri, Asian/damar minyak	*Agathis* spp.
Kauri, Fijian	*Agathis vitiensis*
Kauri, Queensland	*Agathis microstachya*
Lime, European	*Tilia vulgaris*
Mahogany, African	*Khaya ivorensis*
Mahogany, Central American	*Swietenia macrophylla*
Maple, birds'-eye (USA/Canada)	*Acer* spp.
Maple/silkwood, Queensland	*Flindersia breylayana*
Miva mahogany, Australian	*Dysoxylum melleri*
Quandong, Australian silver	*Elaeocarpus grandis*
Rosewood, Australian scented	*Dysoxylon fraseranum*
Rosewood, Brazilian or Rio	*Dalbergia nigra*
Rosewood, New Guinea	*Pterocarpus indicus*
Saffron heart, Australian	*Halfordia kendack*
Sapele	*Entandrophragma cylindricum*
Sitka spruce	*Picea sitchensis*
Sycamore, American	*Platanus* spp.
Teak, Burmese	*Tectona grandis*
Walnut, American black	*Juglans nigra*
Walnut, European	*Juglans regia*
Walnut, Queensland	*Endiandra palmerstonii*

Imperial/metric conversion table
inches to millimetres

inches	mm	inches	mm	inches	mm
⅛	3	9	229	30	762
¼	6	10	254	31	787
⅜	10	11	279	32	813
½	13	12	305	33	838
⅝	16	13	330	34	864
¾	19	14	356	35	889
⅞	22	15	381	36	914
1	25	16	406	37	940
1¼	32	17	432	38	965
1½	38	18	457	39	991
1¾	44	19	483	40	1016
2	51	20	508	41	1041
2½	64	21	533	42	1067
3	76	22	559	43	1092
3½	89	23	584	44	1118
4	102	24	610	45	1143
4½	114	25	635	46	1168
5	127	26	660	47	1194
6	152	27	686	48	1219
7	178	28	711	49	1245
8	203	29	737	50	1270

About the author

Born in Cardiff, Wales, in 1944, Cynthia
Rogers moved to Australia with her family
at the age of six. She left home and
school at 13, and made her living
breaking in horses in central Victoria.
She worked with racehorses and on dairy
farms, and did a stint at share-farming
and herd-testing for a few years.

   She never lost interest in art since she
started drawing with a lump of coal at the
age of four. She spent a lot of time
studying the anatomy of animals and
people; she was always interested in how things were put together, and started making
sculptures of animals. She taught oil painting for 17 years at adult education classes, though
only self-taught herself.

   She spent around 30 years making sculptures in various media – half this time as a
professional sculptor of people, birds, animals and assorted designs for garden ornaments
and other commercial items. She was introduced to woodcarving in 1993 by the 81-year-old
master carver Ben Flack of Brisbane, Australia, and loved it so much that she never went
back permanently to other media. Cynthia won numerous prizes and trophies.

Index

TITLES AVAILABLE FROM
GMC Publications

BOOKS

Woodcarving

Beginning Woodcarving	GMC Publications
Carving Architectural Detail in Wood: The Classical Tradition	Frederick Wilbur
Carving Birds & Beasts	GMC Publications
Carving Classical Styles in Wood	Frederick Wilbur
Carving the Human Figure: Studies in Wood and Stone	Dick Onians
Carving Nature: Wildlife Studies in Wood	Frank Fox-Wilson
Celtic Carved Lovespoons: 30 Patterns	Sharon Littley & Clive Griffin
Decorative Woodcarving (New Edition)	Jeremy Williams
Elements of Woodcarving	Chris Pye
Figure Carving in Wood: Human and Animal Forms	Sara Wilkinson
Lettercarving in Wood: A Practical Course	Chris Pye
Relief Carving in Wood: A Practical Introduction	Chris Pye
Woodcarving for Beginners	GMC Publications
Woodcarving Made Easy	Cynthia Rogers
Woodcarving Tools, Materials & Equipment (New Edition in 2 vols.)	Chris Pye

Woodturning

Bowl Turning Techniques Masterclass	Tony Boase
Chris Child's Projects for Woodturners	Chris Child
Decorating Turned Wood: The Maker's Eye	Liz & Michael O'Donnell
Green Woodwork	Mike Abbott
A Guide to Work-Holding on the Lathe	Fred Holder
Keith Rowley's Woodturning Projects	Keith Rowley
Making Screw Threads in Wood	Fred Holder
Segmented Turning: A Complete Guide	Ron Hampton
Turned Boxes: 50 Designs	Chris Stott
Turning Green Wood	Michael O'Donnell
Turning Pens and Pencils	Kip Christensen & Rex Burningham
Wood for Woodturners	Mark Baker
Woodturning: Forms and Materials	John Hunnex
Woodturning: A Foundation Course (New Edition)	Keith Rowley
Woodturning: A Fresh Approach	Robert Chapman
Woodturning: An Individual Approach	Dave Regester
Woodturning: A Source Book of Shapes	John Hunnex
Woodturning Masterclass	Tony Boase
Woodturning Projects: A Workshop Guide to Shapes	Mark Baker

Woodworking

Beginning Picture Marquetry	Lawrence Threadgold
Carcass Furniture	GMC Publications
Celtic Carved Lovespoons: 30 Patterns	Sharon Littley & Clive Griffin
Celtic Woodcraft	Glenda Bennett
Celtic Woodworking Projects	Glenda Bennett
Complete Woodfinishing (Revised Edition)	Ian Hosker
David Charlesworth's Furniture-Making Technique	David Charlesworth
David Charlesworth's Furniture-Making Techniques – Volume 2	David Charlesworth
Furniture Projects with the Router	Kevin Ley
Furniture Restoration (Practical Crafts)	Kevin Jan Bonner
Furniture Restoration: A Professional at Work	John Lloyd
Furniture Workshop	Kevin Ley
Green Woodwork	Mike Abbott
History of Furniture: Ancient to 1900	Michael Huntley
Intarsia: 30 Patterns for the Scrollsaw	John Everett
Making Heirloom Boxes	Peter Lloyd
Making Screw Threads in Wood	Fred Holder
Making Woodwork Aids and Devices	Robert Wearing
Mastering the Router	Ron Fox
Pine Furniture Projects for the Home	Dave Mackenzie
Router Magic: Jigs, Fixtures and Tricks to Unleash your Router's Full Potential	Bill Hylton
Router Projects for the Home	GMC Publications
Router Tips & Techniques	Robert Wearing
Routing: A Workshop Handbook	Anthony Bailey
Routing for Beginners (Revised and Expanded Edition)	Anthony Bailey
Stickmaking: A Complete Course	Andrew Jones & Clive George
Stickmaking Handbook	Andrew Jones & Clive George
Storage Projects for the Router	GMC Publications
Veneering: A Complete Course	Ian Hosker
Veneering Handbook	Ian Hosker
Wood: Identification & Use	Terry Porter
Woodworking Techniques and Projects	Anthony Bailey
Woodworking with the Router: Professional Router Techniques any Woodworker can Use	Bill Hylton & Fred Matlack

Dolls' Houses and Miniatures

1/12 Scale Character Figures for the Dolls' House	James Carrington
Americana in 1/12 Scale: 50 Authentic Projects	Joanne Ogreenc & Mary Lou Santovec
The Authentic Georgian Dolls' House	Brian Long
A Beginners' Guide to the Dolls' House Hobby	Jean Nisbett
Celtic, Medieval and Tudor Wall Hangings in 1/12 Scale Needlepoint	Sandra Whitehead
Creating Decorative Fabrics: Projects in 1/12 Scale	Janet Storey
Dolls' House Accessories, Fixtures and Fittings	Andrea Barham
Dolls' House Furniture: Easy-to-Make Projects in 1/12 Scale	Freida Gray
Dolls' House Makeovers	Jean Nisbett
Dolls' House Window Treatments	Eve Harwood
Edwardian-Style Hand-Knitted	

An Essential Guide to Bird Photography	Steve Young
Field Guide to Bird Photography	Steve Young
Field Guide to Landscape Photography	Peter Watson
How to Photograph Pets	Nick Ridley
In my Mind's Eye: Seeing in Black and White	Charlie Waite
Life in the Wild: A Photographer's Year	Andy Rouse
Light in the Landscape: A Photographer's Year	Peter Watson
Photographers on Location with Charlie Waite	Charlie Waite
Photographing Wilderness	Jason Friend
Photographing your Garden	Gail Harland
Photography for the Naturalist	Mark Lucock
Photojournalism: An Essential Guide	David Herrod
Professional Landscape and Environmental Photography:	
From 35mm to Large Format	Mark Lucock
Rangefinder	Roger Hicks & Frances Schultz
Underwater Photography	Paul Kay
Where and How to Photograph Wildlife	Peter Evans
Wildlife Photography Workshops	Steve & Ann Toon

Art Techniques

Beginning Watercolours	Bee Morrison
Oil Paintings from the Landscape:	
A Guide for Beginners	Rachel Shirley
Oil Paintings from your Garden:	
A Guide for Beginners	Rachel Shirley
Sketching Landscapes in Pen and Pencil	Joyce Percival

VIDEOS

Drop-in and Pinstuffed Seats	David James
Stuffover Upholstery	David James
Elliptical Turning	David Springett
Woodturning Wizardry	David Springett
Turning Between Centres: The Basics	Dennis White
Turning Bowls	Dennis White
Boxes, Goblets and Screw Threads	Dennis White
Novelties and Projects	Dennis White
Classic Profiles	Dennis White
Twists and Advanced Turning	Dennis White
Sharpening the Professional Way	Jim Kingshott
Sharpening Turning & Carving Tools	Jim Kingshott
Bowl Turning	John Jordan
Hollow Turning	John Jordan

Woodturning: A Foundation Course	Keith Rowley
Carving a Figure: The Female Form	Ray Gonzalez
The Router: A Beginner's Guide	Alan Goodsell
The Scroll Saw: A Beginner's Guide	John Burke

MAGAZINES

Woodturning • Woodcarving

Furniture & Cabinetmaking • The Router

New Woodworking • The Dolls' House Magazine

Outdoor Photography • Black & White Photography

Machine Knitting News • Knitting

Guild Of Master Craftsmen News

The above represents a selection of titles currently published

or scheduled to be published.

All are available direct from the Publishers or through

bookshops, newsagents and specialist retailers.

To place an order, or to obtain a complete catalogue, contact:

GMC Publications,

Castle Place, 166 High Street, Lewes, East Sussex

BN7 1XU United Kingdom

Tel: 01273 488005 Fax: 01273 402866

E-mail: pubs@thegmcgroup.com

Website: www.gmcbooks.com